novum **premium

Tony Jeton Selimi
Multi-Award-Winning, #1 International
Bestselling Author and Consultant

THE
UNFAKEABLE
Code®

**Take Back Control,
Lead Authentically
and Live Freely on
Your Terms.**

*"This is an inspiring, enjoyable, fast-moving book that shows you
how to unlock your full power for unlimited success."*
Brian Tracy, Author, Chairman and CEO of Brian Tracy International

novum premium

This book is also available as e-book.

www.novum-publishing.co.uk

© 2021 novum publishing

ISBN 978-3-99107-385-7
Editing: Hugo Chandler, BA
Cover photos: TJS Cognition Ltd,
Tony Jeton Selimi, Petar Todorov
Cover design, layout & typesetting:
novum publishing
Internal illustrations: TJS Cognition Ltd,
Tony Jeton Selimi

All rights of distribution,
including via film, radio, and television,
photomechanical reproduction,
audio storage media, electronic data
storage media, and the reprinting of
portions of text, are reserved for the
publisher and the author.

Printed in the European Union on
environmentally friendly, chlorine- and
acid-free paper

www.novum-publishing.co.uk.

© 2021 Tony Jeton Selimi (Jeton Tony Selimi)

All rights reserved. No part of this book may be used or reproduced by any means, graphic, electronic, or mechanical, including photocopying, recording, taping or by any information storage retrieval system without the written permission of the author except in the case of brief quotations embodied in critical articles and reviews.

Because of the dynamic nature of the Internet, any web addresses or links contained in this book may have changed since publication and may no longer be valid. The views expressed in this work are solely those of the author and do not necessarily reflect the views of the publisher, and the publisher hereby disclaims any responsibility for them.

The author of this book does not dispense medical advice or prescribe the use of any technique as a form of treatment for physical, emotional, or medical problems without the advice of a physician, either directly or indirectly. The intent of the author is only to offer information of a general nature to help you in your quest for mental, emotional, and spiritual well- being. In the event you use any of the information in this book for yourself, which is your constitutional right, the author and the publisher assume no responsibility for your actions.

Praise for The Unfakeable Code®

"A life manual that assists you in understanding how the Law of Attraction works, and it gives you valuable insights into the science of healing and changing your mindset that will transform your existence." – **Marie Diamond, Global Transformational Teacher, a star from The Secret.**

"Learning how to be truly authentic is a frightening process, yet this book walks you through all aspects of how to move towards this understanding of yourself better and on a deeper level. The Unfakeable Code is an essential guide to becoming a better version of yourself and a great leader by achieving excellence. Tony J. Selimi, offers us a refreshing way to look at authenticity – from objectivity rather than biased opinions of our transient personas.

A fascinating read that's easy to apply to everyday life, and a great book to return to time and time again. The five freedom, experience, and power-enhancing principles will help you build a deeper awareness of all that you are and are not. I recommended it to academics, business owners, leaders, and anyone working in the human development field. Read it cover to cover, over and over, and you too will broaden and deepen the proficiency of your leadership by presenting your most authentic self in every decision you make." – **The Hon Richard Evans, CEO ACE Modular Construction.**

"Tony J. Selimi has proven genius once again in his compilation of all of the intelligence he has assimilated throughout his life, regarding human behaviour and how each one of us can utilise what he shares for the highest good of humankind. The Unfakeable Code® is profoundly touching, personal, and yet, succinct with the body, the mind and the spirit of all. If you've chosen to read this book, then you are on the path to knowing your true authentic self and as Tony says, "Love the unlovable in you."

Tony is a computer all to himself, vibrant and full of intuitive guidance, scientifically proven and logical methods and spiritual techniques are given to you in every page of his book. What you'll find most useful is the compilation of lessons he has learned, the value in the intrinsic cost endured through his journey, and how he turned his pain into an ever-evolving purpose, to travel globally, consulting and creating brilliant leaders in the world. You'll feel blessed to have his genius displayed in the written word with his personal touch, which only he can relay, all that he has gained; by being in the positions life has afforded him, the challenges, the accomplishments and the love factor that he has always displayed to those of us privileged enough to work with him and to know him.

His heart is pure, and you will see this in the writing of this offering to you who are wishing to know more about self. If you are looking for an authoritative guide to uncovering the real you, the person you know so little about, but is indelibly inscribed within you, then distribute copies of Tony's book to everyone you know.

His teachings are illuminating the path to humanity's growth, by revealing the predicaments we find ourselves in, the answers to knowing our spiritual intelligence within, and how to not only to understand it but to know it and use it to be all that we can be in this life. His ways of expression are nothing less than the brilliance and fullness of love, encouragement and support for you to grow, grow, grow. Knowing oneself has never been presented so brilliantly before." – **Tammy De Mirza Rosado, Author, Relationship Expert and an Intuitive known as The Freedom Alchemist.**

"WOW! Bringing the unconscious to the conscious. The Unfakeable Code's five life-transforming principles are a guide to a more complete and confident life. It enables you to explore your inner-self and your relationship with your soul. Be ready for an immersive experience that will awaken your life by finding the freedom of authenticity." – **Daniel Nikolla, Multi-Award-Winning Marketing Manager.**

"Do you feel a gap between who you are and who you think you should be? Is your soul screaming to be rescued giving you the urge to unmask yourself and to be the authentic you that you were made to be? If so, in every chapter of this book, you'll learn how the essence of authenticity is yourself entirely. It requires courage, something many people lack.

Tony J. Selimi makes a convincing case for being authentic; to be a daily decision, and that there is no substitute for doing the work. Rather than vague concepts and lofty clichés, he dives deep into the complex nuances of real authenticity. This book serves as a life manual for those who want to do the work and own their power. Read it if you intend to be who you are born to be – and then read it, again and again, to grow into all you can imagine, with authenticity leading the way. If you are looking for a life manual to unlock your potential, then this book is for you, your children, family, business and every employee in your business." – **Rezijana Saiti, Attorney at Law.**

"In this life-changing book, The Unfakeable Code®, the well-known author gives us practical ways to be more authentic; to take off the mask, and show our real self to the world, no matter who we are and what we do. A considerable and well-deserved place is given to knowing, managing and understanding the role that emotions and Emotional Intelligence play in our lives. Based on the newest outcomes from the field of Neuroleadership and Neuroscience, till now, its impact on every aspect of our lives has been underestimated.

This book is didactically well designed, and messages are formulated with powerful insights, which you can apply everywhere and any time. Tony's style and language are easy to understand and keep the reader engaged and inflow. As an international scientist and professor of Leadership and Emotional Intelligence, I strongly suggest that everyone should read this book. If you have a leadership position, this book is a must for you, as it helps you to enhance your leadership competencies. If you are a parent, it serves you on how to behave as a role model for your children.

If you are a student or an employee, it helps you to achieve the grip on your aspiring position you want. If you are self-employed, it serves you to strengthen your self-confidence and self-esteem to overcome all barriers towards growing your business. Thank you, dear Tony J. Selimi, for giving the world such an insightful book, which undoubtedly will change millions of lives for good. Wishing you all the best in all your activities towards enhancing well-being and wealth-being of the humankind." – **Prof. Dr Fadil Çitaku, PhD, MME (Uni Bern), founder and CEO of the Academy of Leadership Sciences Switzerland.**

"We lead lives of quiet desperation. The world we live in now seems to become more volatile, uncertain, complicated, and ambiguous each day. What can we do? Grab your copy of The Unfakeable Code® and read it over and over again. The headnote by Tony J. Selimi is probably what Oscar Wilde had in mind when he suggested, "Be yourself. Everyone else is taken." Indeed, Tony concludes with these thoughts, "Let love be your first choice, and daily choose to live in grace and gratitude." Being an authentic individual is about integrating all of our transient personas into the unfakeable individual we were born to be.

The process does involve tough choices and hard work. When determining who you are in your way and making the contributions that only you can make. Tony's words of guidance provide you with both insight and wisdom. You will come to acknowledge how only those with integrity will be blessed by the powers of your authentic individual being revealed as you remove the mask you show to the world. Remember to have fun, though, and savour those virtue buzzes along the way. Truly inspirational. Must read." – **Lisa White, Senior Product Manager, Dial A Flight.**

"The Unfakeable Code® is full of insightful examinations into the value of taking back control, upgrading one's psychology, and being authentic in all of your endeavours. Tony reveals an immediately useful mind-upgrading model of authenticity that enables you to replace habitual reactions with authentic ones that stand by your values, while still making effective business decisions. The book is written in an easy to follow style; this makes it accessible to a broad audience. I therefore highly recommend this book to business owners, leaders, and anyone interested in living, leading, loving and succeeding with authenticity and integrity." – **Georgi Milushev, Program Manager, Amazon.**

"The Unfakeable Code® is an awakening, enlightening, and inspirational motivation we have all been searching for. It is a book which, every single one of us can resonate with; no matter from, or what gender, race or backgrounds we come from or what beliefs we hold.

Tony begins the book by describing his childhood and baring all the struggles he had, for all of us to read and be a part of. This has made the book come alive for me. The way he has highlighted the difficulties he had to face and endure and the way he overcame them all makes the reader able to relate to those problems. However, he also provides a sense of hope that anyone can overcome such challenges.

Every single one of us has a fake identity as Tony proclaims in his book. We are all a mixture of good and bad, powerful and vulnerable – we all possess these qualities. Tony expands beautifully on how we can love ourselves for who we are, embrace all our qualities and how to improve ourselves; but at the same time be more understanding to others who have yet reached a balance and accepted themselves fully, with love.

A genuinely brilliant yet daring book that motivates the reader to question him or herself, delve deeper into who we are, and it encourages them to do it boldly and without regrets. In a world where virtual reality has become more powerful than the living truth, I am confident that every reader will be able to find themselves while reading this book, which I would classify as a gem standing proud amongst all the other self-discovery books." – **Dr Elgerta Ismaili, NHS England.**

"Authenticity is something we all have to deal with throughout our lives. When I was younger, I used to live in the illusion that this is something we only have to do once, or perhaps a few times, like for example, coming out of the closet. Still, our beings and our lives are by far more complex. An inquisitive and self-reflective mind might notice some layers of qualities, thoughts and behaviours which we keep hidden to others, or even to ourselves, but it often takes the help of a skilled external observer to act as a mirror and help us to dig deeper.

For the last few years, I've had the privilege to be working with Tony as my life and business coach. In the journey, learning and applying Tony's revolutionary teachings, I have discovered and overcome many perceived obstacles to my authenticity. I have therefore been eager to read the crystallisation of his teachings in the five life-changing principles contained in this book The Unfakeable Code®.

Whether you are entirely new to this or a veteran in personal development, let Tony's capable mixture of narrative, detailed teachings and personal anecdotes patiently guide you through the structure of this manual and help you rediscover, express and live a life more and more aligned with your authentic self." – **Dr. Pietro Emanuele Garbelli, Acute Physician, Founder of Purposefully Transforming Healthcare®.**

"From the moment you meet Tony, you feel infused with a feeling of love like never before. After interviewing him a few times on London Albanian Radio, I decided to book a consultation to help me with some specific health and professional issues I was experiencing. In the two-hour session, my core beliefs were challenged, changed and realigned like never before. I felt an opening in my heart that no other life coach, mentor and healer has ever achieved before.

His award-winning and #1 bestselling books A Path to Wisdom and #Loneliness sparked many enlightening radio conversations on different topics that my audience from around the world loved. He changed me and the lives of the millions of people through the enlightening perspectives he shares in talks, seminars, consulting and healing sessions, and his Living My Illusion documentary. I am blessed to have had the opportunity to be an early reviewer of his new book The Unfakeable Code®, as I knew it would be another pearl he is gifting to humanity.

Each of the five principles is a life-transforming personal journey that masterfully guides you to discover your inner universe, learn how to take back your power, and let (as Tony beautifully describes it in the book) your authentic, and unfakeable being lead the way. I recommend reading each sentence with heightened awareness, for if you let them, they will heal your body, mind and soul. He teaches you how to upgrade your mind, language, and use values to help you master your false self-persona, raise your self-esteem, and be a confident leader of yourself and others. In every chapter, you can review all aspects of your life, from family, friends, relationships to business and financial aspects.

As you perform every exercise, you will start to awaken dormant parts of yourself by showering you with the gift of clarity, the joy of life, and wisdom, and will give you the strength and courage you need to face every difficulty with dignity and serenity. I invite you to emerge your being in another universe and discover how to unleash your unfakeable being's authentic power which will help you to live freely on your terms." – **Anila Gremi Kushova, Radio Presenter, Diplomacy and International Affairs Expert.**

"If you are looking for a book that can help you take back control of the direction your life is going in and succeed in life with authenticity, then The Unfakeable Code® is the book for you. Tony J. Selimi shows you an incredible system to safely peel off the masks of your wounded persona that were created through inner discord, pain, and that lonely feeling within us that manifests in various forms in our society. A must-read book for today's modern leader, business owner, and citizen living in a technological Disneyland, yearning for connection, love, and fulfilment." – **Patryk Wezowski, Award-winning Film Maker, Director, Producer, Record-breaking Fundraising Expert.**

"You may never be at peace with others if you are at war with yourself," says the author – a straightforward sentence, yet very powerful and sophisticated. Simple: – All of us are at war with ourselves! Complex: – Not an easy solution! Powerful: –Tony J. Selimi provides the tools! No matter what we have been through in life or how far we have travelled. Frequently we feel like we are standing at a crossroads, as though our purpose in life has vanished and that we have lost control of our steering wheel.

Then somebody like Tony enters our lives with a book like The Unfakeable Code® and yes! it shakes your foundation to the core, but at the same time, it's another painful and beautiful wake-up call for our sleepy souls.

Apply the five rules! Be authentic! Stop the inner war …

Only a mastermind like Tony J. Selimi can harmonise science, psychology and spirituality with such simplicity and brilliance. This is a book that will unstick any reader from a worthlessness mentality or a lack of confidence state, while adding more soul, value or revenue to all the businesses, advanced entrepreneurs and people of all profiles from different walks of life. This book is another priceless gift to humanity!" – **Dije Berdynaj, Director of Sales at Hampton Resorts and Hospitality, Southampton, New York.**

"This book is creative, engaging, and persuasive. Tony J. Selimi has once again succeeded in dissecting different aspects of our transient personas, examining both our magnificence and our deficiencies, the negative and the constructive potentialities of our deceptive nature, and gives you ten mind upgrading principles that will awaken the authentic power of your unfakeable individual.

Tony's objective is to self-investigate the real positive nature of showing confidently showing the world your true self. The book is clearly written and so easy to follow, which makes it accessible to a broad audience. I therefore highly recommend this book to consultants, students, teachers, people from all professions, business owners and leaders – especially those who suffer from Obsessive Compulsive Disorder (OCD) or other mental health-related issues." – **Paul McMonagle, Piping Supervisor, Workbacks Engineer, and an Ambassador for Mental Health.**

"Tony's take on authenticity is both thought-provoking and practical. With ten simple to understand mind elevating principles, he demystifies what authenticity is, and importantly what it is not, in order to take back control and own our power. He is one of the best storytellers of our time who brings you teachings and research from science and client's experience driven research to life; using real stories about real people, set in a conversational tone that has you on the edge of your seat, gasping in amazement at how accurately each example applies to your life experiences and leadership style.

The Unfakeable Code® is a straightforward book about the hard work it takes to become a truly authentic individual, but it's also about the rewards of making that investment." – **Marija Milushev, International Compliance Analyst, Chicago.**

"The hunger for authenticity guides us throughout our lives. As a cardiologist working in the NHS, I read a lot of self-help books to help me cope better with burnout, stress, and to communicate authentically and mindfully with patients, their families, junior doctors and my superiors. But Tony J. Selimi's book The Unfakeable Code® is a "master class" in attaining freedom and becoming successful while and through attending to one's unfakeable true self. With clear language, the five-step principles, and compelling metaphors, he explores the complexities of personal psychology and the quirks of spiritual challenges; melding these together thoughtfully and provocatively.

Selimi has once again pioneered a formula for living freely on your terms, drawing on the solid science of balanced psychology to develop gold-standard principles for assessing authenticity. He reveals that when people integrate their disowned personas, they naturally begin to examine themselves psychologically, accommodate new information and live more authentically. I recommend it to my fellow healthcare professionals, entrepreneurs, business owners, executives and aspiring executives who dare to look at themselves as well as others, with objectivity. Because Selimi presents dozens of examples of his consulting conversations, I also recommend it to fellow professionals who wish to learn from a masterful teacher." – **Dr. Sc. Todorche Stamenov, NHS London.**

"A unique book that helps you to ask questions of yourself that you have never dared to ask before. If you follow the principles of Tony's teachings, your life could turn drastically from living according to other people's expectations to an authentic, balanced and self-expressing experience. This book is a gift to your soul, and it opens up multiple possibilities to a whole new way of thinking, living and being. A must-read for everyone on a self-discovery journey! Go on, take the best adventure of your life yet! Your soul, mind and heart will thank you for it!" – **Timea Van der Molen, Company Director – Vandercom Films.**

"In this extraordinary and powerful book, Tony J. Selimi lays out the path to authenticity and true self-fulfilment, with unyielding clarity and a unique synthesis of science, spirit, personal experience and psychology. In the five central principles, he shows that the attraction of our times for the fakeable and inauthentic, for facades and props, for making our lives reliant on the judgments and expectations of others (or what we think are their expectations) leads us to the dead-end of self-deception and blind egotism.

One of my favourite aspects of the book is that this state of endless dissatisfaction can be recorded by the brain and be replaced by new daily habits, almost step by step, to rewire our "models of reality" and rediscover our essential, authentic self. This book is a charter for reprogramming your life and making a higher level, re-energised contribution to the real world around you and the people within it." **Dr. David Clive Price, Mental Wellbeing Mentor and Author of Hidden Demons.**

"This book is an excellent introduction to the thought of the great contemporary British-Albanian global educator, philosopher, healer and spiritual teacher Tony J. Selimi, whose integrated work helped me heal my psoriasis and transform our business. Written to inspire everyone in the shared struggle to be true to oneself, and meet ever-increasing daily demands, The

Unfakeable Code® sheds light on an action plan for making more mindful and conscious choices. Tony masterfully guides you into the awareness that being authentic is more than just making the right ethical decisions.

It is a daily choice to do the work to integrate your transient personas into one genuine, unfakeable individual. His ten mind-enhancing and life-transforming simple yet extremely effective principles open up possibilities for being successful when making small, everyday decisions. I therefore highly recommend this book to fellow business owners, parents, educators, consultants, and every woman interested in knowing how to take back control and live life freely on their terms." – **Albana Osmani, Entrepreneur and Restaurateur, London.**

"I am so happy I got the opportunity to read The Unfakeable Code®, as I have always been interested in how the brain and our body works together. If you are looking to learn how to take back control, have a healthy body-mind-soul connection and consciously create an inspired life, then this book is must-read. It gives you an understanding of how your mind was programmed in the past, by the people you have surrounded yourself with, and how by using the five-principles Tony has masterfully put together the way you can reprogram your mind to achieve any life outcome you want with authenticity leading the way." – **Ib Nielsen, Health Entrepreneur, Zinzino, Denmark.**

"When invited to review The Unfakeable Code®, I jumped at the opportunity to uncover the golden Tony's golden nuggets. Initially, on ploughing through the names of the other reviewers, I questioned whether I was the right person? Wow, how wrong was I, Tony has this innate ability to align you with your sense of self. Each word touched a core within me – brilliant. In essence, the works and practices of Tony J. Selimi will continue to resonate, help and guides humankind across the globe as we face each daily challenges. The book is the best gift you can give yourself. Thank you for sharing your wealth." – **Sue Bannister, Client, Author of "No Sugar My Journey My Choice" and "Rope's Adventures on the 'High Seas'."**

"To personally meet Tony J. Selimi is a blessing, for he will infuse your DNA with love and wisdom. His book, The Unfakeable Code®, offers you a simple way to use tools for everyday life. The five life-enhancing principles help you to enter into your consciousness, to develop all your mental faculties, and to get to know who you are and who you are not. It is a life handbook each one of us can use to make informed choices, decisions and question our transient personas that hide our authentic nature.

The step by step instructions teaches you about how the process of harmonising body, mind and spirit is the key to liberating your entire intelligence. As someone with loads of managerial responsibilities, the book serves me to develop my leadership skills further. It takes one far beyond the emotional intelligence principles, into the world where your unfakeable self uses your material and spiritual intelligence to work with you and for you.

As a father of two, the book helps me to act as a role model for my children. It also helps me, of course, to bring up my children using balanced psychology, and to have a healthy and love-infused relationship with my wife. As my uncle and godfather of our daughter Jannah, Tony's wisdom and love energises our everyday life. After every phone call or WhatsApp message, a big spark of energy jumps over to the family and inspires me to be more. I thank you, Tony J. Selimi, for enduring the pain, investing all you had in all you have become, and giving billions of people such an inspiring book that changes you forever and for better." – **Adrian Dalipi, Stv Leiter Abteilung Sonderbewilligung, Switzerland.**

"Tony J. Selimi's The Unfakeable Code® provides a true inspiration and motivation to live life on an exciting level. He emphasises that there are no shortcuts, no substitutes, no playing safe if you want to be the true you, and be the leader of your life.

He makes you understand that there is no more significant loss than not discovering your talents, amazingness and self-worth. Still, there is no more exceptional beauty than complete knowledge of your true self and the power of your being. Read, understand and implement his proposed principles and be bold, be authentic, be the inspiration, simply be the most you can be! He has done it!

And as Tony beautifully conveys, the world needs your uniqueness, your essence and it cannot unfold into its spectacular fullness without you. It's a brilliant read that will challenge you, give you hope and guide you to your greatness." – **Yola Nash, MS. WABC Radio Host New York City, Singer, Producer.**

"Refreshing, insightful and empowering, Tony has a talent for helping you remember that life itself is a gift. If you want to experience more alignment, purpose and visible results in this universe, Tony and his books will guide you there, plus show you how to awaken your own unique, authentic path.

Like "A Path to Wisdom", his book The Unfakeable Code® illuminates steps to take to reclaim direction in your life by asking the right questions that in turn will reveal the answers and guidance that will make your heart sing.

Tony J. Selimi encourages you from a place of objectivity and experience to embark on this journey inward. Pick up a copy to discover the exciting treasure hunt that awaits, and let Tony remind you that YOU are the treasure." – **Michael André Ford, Angel Intuitive.**

"Albert Einstein famously said that doing the same thing over and over again and expecting different results is insanity. Tony's book is a brilliant manual for a journey out of this insanity! The Unfakeable Code® will guide you with great clarity towards allowing yourself to live from the truth of your being. What a wonderful message for this spiritual upgrade, so essential for living a deeply satisfying life." – **Fella Cederbaum, Award-winning Filmmaker, Composer, Poet and Author of "Of Life and Other Such Matters".**

"The hidden problem with fake-it-till-you-make-it is that you usually don't realise until it's too late that you are strengthening fakery, which is ultimately based on a fear that you are not good enough. Held in place by lies, when you take that live or online, you amplify the very things you are trying to conceal. The delusion is thinking you have pulled off the illusion; that no one noticed.

The reality, even if you fool everybody, is that you have not fooled yourself unless you are a sociopath, a pathological liar or a 24-carat gold plated narcissist – where you are so far out of alignment that you contemptuously believe that people are stupid, and that they deserve to be lied to. If you are in doubt, err on the side of self-honesty. It is better to enjoy a modicum of authentic success than superficial adulation and reputational damage. Tony Selimi's new book The Unfakeable Code® is your essential guide to a truly authentic life." – **Andrew Priestley Grad Dip Psych, B. Ed, Leadership Mentor, Bestselling Author, Founder of The Coaching Experience.**

"The Unfakeable Code® and the five mind-upgrading principles are so perfect in these uncertain times. In each chapter, Tony J. Selimi speaks of his journey as he offers concrete steps and guidance on living an authentic life; a life to thrive, love, listen, connect and to create a vision from within to achieve your highest potential. It is highly recommended for anyone in the personal development world for expanding greater self-awareness and the presence of the authentic self." – **Shelley J. Whitehead, Relationship, Dating and Bereavement Expert.**

"Incredibly, this is an educational life manual that gives fruitful ideas to vertical thinkers for the conception of harmonising material and heart intelligence, which is something many of us think is insurmountable and too far-fetched to dwell-on in our day to day lives." – **Jack Canfield, America's #1 Success Coach.**

Contents

Foreword 27

Introduction –
What is The Unfakeable Code®? 31

Take Off the Mask; Your Soul is Waiting 53
Principle #1:
To Unmask Yourself Is to Know Thyself. 53
  Break the Illusion of a One-sided
  Positive or Negative Persona 58
  Change the Thoughts You Think,
  Words You Speak and the Language You Use 65
  Know What Truly Stops You from
  Taking Off your Illusory Masks 81

Rewire Your Existential Models of Reality 87
Principle #2:
Stop Working to Survive, Wake-Up and Thrive 87
  The Choices You Make Determines
  the Reality You Create 90
  When Trust Dies, Mistrust Blossoms 96
  Stop Being a People Pleaser 99
Transform Your Scarcity Persona
into a Thriving Individual 104

Disarm Your Emotions 107
Principle #3:
Disarm Your Emotional Field to Build
an Impenetrable Shield 107
  Stop Being a Slave to Your One-sided Emotions 110
  See Emotional Crisis as a Blessing in Disguise 112

*What Does Your Relationship with
Food Say About You?* 117
Master Your Emotions and Save a Life 120

Stop Giving Your Power Away, Own it 123
Principle #4:
Taking Back Control is an Inside Job 123
*Mirror, Mirror on the Wall,
Whose More Controlling of Them All?* 124
Adopt Pain and Pleasure in Equal Measure Attitude 127
*Don't Be Convinced By Your Arguments,
But By Your Sincerity* 132
Go from Doing to Undoing 136
Your Life is an Expression of Your Consciousness 142

Master the Virtue of Loving Prudently 150
Principle #5:
Choose Love as Your Military Commander
that Wins Every Battle in Life 150
*Demystify Your Idea of What Love Should be,
Must be, and is* 154
When Judgment Goes, Love Appears 161
In Letting Go, You Let Love in 170
Love Yourself, as Everyone Else is Taken 175
Let Your Authenticity Shape Your Destiny 183

**Who Can Benefit from Using
The Unfakeable Code®?** 189

What next? 190

Acknowledgements 195

About the Author 201

Transformational Products 205
A Path to Wisdom 205
#Loneliness: The Virus of Modern Age 208
Fit for Purpose Leadership #3 211
Living My Illusion – The Truth Hurts Multi-Award
Coaching Documentary 213
TJS Evolutionary Meditation Solutions® 216
Vital Planning for Elevated Living 219

Notes 221

This book is dedicated to:

My loved ones: Dr. Sc. Todorche Stamenov, my late parents Shaqir and Ljutvije Selimi, grandparents Akik and Satka Selimi, and Sinan and Hava Tafai. My incredible sisters and their husbands Feleknaz and Xhavit Dalipi, Hanumsha and Besir Jusufi, Selime Selimi, Drita and Aziz Osmani, and my brother Selim and his wife, Flora Selimi. My nieces Adelina, Rezijana, Valdeta, Besa, Arjeta, Bernadeta, Deliza, and my nephews Ardijan, Berat, Elzan, Rinim, Ardit and Arijan. My grandnephews and grandnieces, Doa, Tara, Almira, Erion, Ali, Fatima, Erin, Edon, Noar, especially Janna, to whom Todor and I have the honour of being her godparents. To my extended family Vanče and his late wife Mirjanka Stamenov, Marija, Georgi and Marco Milushev, Radica Strahilova whose presence and support have enriched my heart.

You, the visionary entrepreneur, business owner, and leader who seeks authenticity as a way to be more engaged, inspired, and productive. The curious father, mother, son, daughter, and friend who is ready to take back control of the direction your life is going in, to make dreams happen with authenticity. My worldwide friends, clients, students and fans who seek to learn new ways of thinking, living and being, that not only can skyrocket your fulfilment in every critical area of life, but also to help you grow your worth and live freely on your own terms. Those of you who are truth seekers, educators, and health professionals in search of innovative solutions to ever-growing global problems.

The growth-hungry individuals who want to harmonise material and spiritual intelligence and awaken yourselves to a life of unprecedented achievements, freedom, and success; those who are ready to awaken dormant parts of your magnificent being, upgrade your psychology to recover pathways to unleashing the power of your unfakeable nature, and embrace universal truths and the wholeness existing in the oneness paradigm.

All of you who through self-help want to inspire decisive action and life-changing transformation in others, with authenticity leading the way. Those of you who seek a way out of an unwanted situation and consciously want to create extraordinary life experiences, where you feel accepted and loved for what you are and are not, who want to expand your awareness through self-mastery, and loving those disowned parts of your being that you judge and disassociate yourself with.

Lastly, to my spirit, who volunteered for this assignment, and continues to guide me to its ongoing unfolding and fruition.

Foreword

I have had the opportunity to teach about the significance and the power of being authentic which is key, a rewarding component of Tony J. Selimi's inspiring mission of helping others. Now you can understand the benefits of leading by example while living fully and authentically. Being authentic far outweighs the risks of you being vulnerable by living behind facades and being seen as somehow different than the person you truly are. Tony's new book The Unfakeable Code® is a godsend to those who want to live, make a difference and be loved for who they truly are.

Drawing on the wisdom of existential and other philosophers, the insights and research of psychologists, and case studies from his own client experiences, Tony shows you how authenticity is the foundation of human happiness and development. Selimi presents his fresh and inspiring perspective on the psychology of authenticity, alongside practical advice and exercises for you, the reader.

Once again, Tony has managed to write an inspired book that takes you into an inside out luminous reality of connectivity at every level of existence, to recover pathways to authenticity, and a deep understanding of the role your transient masked personas play in your unfakeable individual's ever-evolving purpose in life. With great delicacy, he uses objectivity to awaken his readers' awareness of the interconnectedness that is present in all life.

It is a compelling compilation of fascinating life learnings, experiences, and enthralling discoveries that awaken you to the authentic power you possess within. It is a power that is not given to you by degrees and awards you attain, or how much money you make, but one that comes from letting your authentic being lead the way.

It is only in the deceptive façades of our various transient personas that we separate the inseparable, divide the indivisible, and polarise the unpolarizable. Tony provides us with a code consisting of five life-transforming principles for consciously creating a more favourable reality, in which you exercise your freedom of choice. In each of the five principles, you'll find the wisdom that strengthens and upgrade your mental faculties, unleashes your authentic power, and helps you to grow your material and spiritual wealth.

He has captured the deceptive nature of our false ego-self, and introduce it in such a concise and sophisticated manner as to leave the reader fully empowered to take control of the direction they want their life to go.

This timely and significant book is the life manual to unlocking your intrinsic worth, to grow your authentic power, and lead in business, personal or professional life with authenticity. You can use the principles shared to become more confident, connected, capable, and more credible and fulfilled in your day-to-day existence.

The book is filled with his own and other individual's real-life stories, powerful metaphors and anecdotes, and drawing upon spiritual traditions and teachings, science, technology, and modern psychology. The Unfakeable Code® is a timely guide to assist you safely and authentically through unchartered business, personal and professional territories, to help you install a new code that your mind can use to get from where you are now to where you want to be.

Be prepared to go deep within, answer many questions and get to the root cause of your perceived challenges. Get ready to unveil what the hidden motives are behind the façades you show to the world. To tackle the real source of your inner discord, identify crises and the lack of material wealth in your life. As you reach the end of the book, you'll be left feeling uplifted, inspired, and empowered to take on any life challenge that may be blocking your way to reaching your most inspired goals.

As you complete answering the question posed to you in each chapter, you will be left with awe at how easy it is to change your circumstances and own your power. Tony shows you masterfully how small invisible changes in the way you think can visibly upgrade your psychology, change the way you behave, and build your confidence to be all you can become.

The more you apply the principles shared in each chapter, the more you will start to see life through a lens of objectivity, and the more in control of your emotions and freedom you will become. You will begin to access, integrate, acknowledge and listen to the messages that come from within your most authentic being.

Give yourself the best gift you could wish for, and read this book multiple times from cover to cover, to help you turn the chaos in your inner world into the order you want in your outer world. The author has simplified the authenticity topic for every ordinary person to read, digest, and use.

In integrating as many traits of your disowned personas as you can, you too will give rise to an authentic individual who easily accesses the abundance, opportunities and the infinite wisdom that resides inside you.

The journey that this book takes you is one of unlocking your authentic inner power, reviving your senses, and helping you consciously create more material and spiritual wealth. In doing so, you will feel more in control of the choices and the freedom you want to create in your life.

Each chapter will guide you to access the tacit knowledge that already exists in your body, mind, heart, and soul; to create and implement the changes, the shifts, and the transformation you are seeking to make, with learning to love prudently and communicating mindfully.

This book is fascinating, original and persuasive. Selimi succeeds in dissecting different aspects of our transient personas, screening both its grandeur and its deficiencies, both the so-called destructive and constructive potentialities of a moral ideal not being taken seriously, as an important factor shaping our authenticity.

The author's objective is to persuade you, the reader, to investigate the pure and robust nature of being an inwardly authentic individual that, though seemingly already corrupted by transient outer personas, is still present deep within us. He makes the unleashing of our authentic power a critical and essential step in influencing how we shape our experiences in life.

Tony, once again, you have cared, dared, loved, and shared a timely and transcendent message for the sake of all of us who are inexplicably bonded across the world.

Dr. John Demartini, Human Behavioural Specialist, Educator, International best-selling Author and Founder of the Demartini Institute.

Introduction –
What is The Unfakeable Code®?

"What limits your freedom is what you think you know that isn't true." – Tony J. Selimi

Are you an Unfakeable individual? Or would you rather be a copy?

Today, many of us buy into the myth that wearing a mask is better than being authentic, that only certain people can succeed, and that to change your life, you have to develop positive psychology. This unhealthy way of thinking is encouraged even more now given how uncertain people and the world of business are. If you're already someone who subscribes to a "biased thinking" way of thinking, then this book is going to shake things up for you.

The notion of being an authentic individual will become clearer throughout this inspired book comprising five mind-upgrading, life-enhancing, and business-transforming principles that are interrelated and interdependent. You will be taken on a self-awareness journey of the role your transient identities, the self-deceptive masked persona you show to the world, the unbiased processing of information, appropriate transparency, objectivity and concordance among behaviour, intuition and values play in how free, successful, and fulfilled you become in life.

Each of the five principles and their associated ideas, which are fully explained in every chapter of this book may just irreversibly disrupt your most deeply held beliefs about you, your work, your success, and, indeed, your life. The exercises presented will help you comprise authenticity in every critical area of life. You will develop a depth of understanding about your mind, or as psychologists like to say, context, and about how adopting the strategies shared, you can successfully upgrade your mind's code as often as you update your apps on your smartphone.

There is some work that, being authentic you would prefer not to do but, yes, you do it because you are true to your values and live them every moment, naturally. You have to roll up your sleeves and do whatever must be done as well as you can.

You may be wondering daily who you are, what are you here to do, and why you behave the way you do. Perhaps, after you've taken a selfie, that you shared on your Instagram, put on that Dolce Gabbana suit, your favourite Chanel dress, or covered yourself with makeup, you might stare at yourself in the mirror, contemplating who your authentic self truly is.

You may ponder, over what is it that makes you put on a mask, be dishonest with others, and feel like you have no control over your emotional reaction to external events. You may ponder over what makes your deceptive nature so powerful that you end up being a slave to your egotistical, sceptical and selfish character.

Incredulous?

Perhaps yes, and maybe not. I invite you to entertain the possibility that the part of you that is Unfakeable is there to daily nudge you to wake up, and to help you correct your course in life. In other words, do you think your current view of who you are is large enough to allow for subtle, intuitive, extraordinary or unusual experiences? Or does your self-deceptive persona discount them automatically?

Since I can remember, I was always curious about life. Who or what created all the animals, us, and where in the universe we come from? From a very young age, my parents taught me fair-minded values that, to date, have played a crucial role in my ever-evolving life. They also instilled in me the importance that education, integrity, and service to others play in bettering our lives, the society we live in, and the world in general.

As I started to form my own opinions about life, which sometimes contradicted those of my parents, the culture and the society I lived in, I needed to come up with a way to express myself authentically, without fear of judgement, ridicule and shame. I needed to be able to write letters containing secret messages to friends that only I and the intended recipient could understand.

So, I came up with a few secret codes to keep the information hidden so neither my parent's nor my friend's parents could understand. For instance, I would replace the letters of a word with numbers or symbols, following a particular set of rules. For my friend on the other end to understand the message, he or she would need to know the code and apply the same set of rules, in reverse, to figure out what I had written.

The penny about how our ability to code and decode messages is part of our makeup dropped for me in high school when, in one of my biology classes, we started to learn about our genetic code. The set of rules by which information encoded in our genetic material (DNA or RNA sequences) is translated into proteins (amino acid sequences) by living cells. I realised then how decoding messages is also an essential step in gene expression and the process in which information from a gene is used to construct a protein (or other functional products).

As it turns out, the way our brain processes information is no different, in fact, in many ways, it does the same thing. To make sense of the billions of pieces of information it receives through our five senses from our inner and outer world, it needs to filter, classify, delete, code, and decode data.

Each chapter is written in such a way for you to take a closer look at how, just like your genes, your way of expressing and processing data in your brain is unique.; and how, by using The Unfakeable Code's five mind upgrading principles, you can transcend old models of thinking, question the gibberish rules, and rewire your models of reality so that you can consciously create the freedom and the life that you want, upgrade your psychology, re-examine your values, beliefs, actions and behaviours, and be more of the authentic, unfakeable individual you were born to be.

Why? – because the vast majority of your mind's code is encoded with the same system as your parents and the environment in which you were born. I often refer to it as the canonical mind code, or merely the inherited general code. Forgetting that your brain can create and run many variant codes; it is why I know that the more you apply what you will be learning throughout this book, the more growth you'll experience.

What those principles can help you achieve is unique to you. Why? – because there is no one else in the world who thinks the way you think, you are authentic. So is your mind's programming, the code it runs and the hierarchy of your values that drives your attitudes, behaviours, choices, and decisions can either break or make you.

Just the way researchers needed to figure out how to crack the genetic code, it's up to you to invest the time to read, re-read, and keep applying the principles shared daily in every chapter to create, break, and upgrade your mind's code.

Why this is a big problem for you?

Because you are born with the ability to do both evil and good; what you choose when war rages inside or outside you is what defines who you become; and, in one of the most straightforward potential mind's codes, each belief, thought, and value you have injected into your persona might correspond to one dis-empowered action, toxic behaviour, and wrong decision that could ruin your business, personal or professional life. Remember, a healthy mind leads to a healthy body and an inspired destiny.

If you want to take back control, be more confident, and more satisfied you need a mind code that breaks the cycle of the fearful, not good enough, controlling, weak and scarcity persona that may be running your life.

However, upgrading your psychology cannot work unless you are consistent, committed, and persistent. The reason for that is because you will never be at peace with others if you are at war with yourself.

You may or may not know that the average person has about 12,000 to 70,000 thoughts per day. And, of those, 80% are negative, and 95% are the same repetitive thoughts as the day before. Thus, the installing of your unfakeable code into your mind involves something more complicated than a one-to-one matching of beliefs, emotions, thoughts and values, and so does the cracking of it.

The idea to create The Unfakeable Code® started in my early teenage years when my father bought me my first computer, the ZX-Spectrum. I was fascinated by it. What made it even more exciting was the fact that no one in Gostivar, the town in the Northern Republic of Macedonia that I grew up in, in the early '80s knew anything about computers. I was the cool kid who could pull electronic equipment apart, put it back together, and program my computer to perform essential mathematical functions. I became a master at being able to write various codes and even write a program to display limited graphics.

The year after, my father got me my Commodore 64, and as soon as the Commodore 128 came out, he ensured I had that one too. I was fascinated to learn the Basic, Fortran, Pascal and Cobol computer languages. I enjoyed playing video games that came pre-recorded on cassettes and I even created my own version of the famous game PAC-MAN.

Knowing that Rade Jovčevski Korčagin was the top maths and science high school in what was then the Socialist Republic of Macedonia, I convinced my parents to send me there to study, despite the fact that the material and teaching was not in my native Albanian language.

I spent the summer of 1984 perfecting my Macedonian language, and in late August, at the age of 14, I moved to Skopje, the capital city. I started to live alone, away from my family in a studio apartment that my parents had bought for my sister and I to pursue higher education. I was over the moon. From the kitchen windows you could see the busy Karposh boulevard, and I had an outside space where I put flowers that came from my parent's garden. The flat was in one of the concrete architecture communist-era apartment blocks situated in the city zone called Karposh II, and about thirty minutes bus ride from my new high school. I felt freer than ever.

We had an hour allocated weekly for computer studies wherein we learnt about how IBM computers were built, programmed and how they could be used personally or in business. At night, when all of the school teachers and students had gone home, I would bribe the cleaners with sweets to let me continue studying in the computer room until they had finished cleaning the whole school and were ready to go home.

Four years passed by very quickly. By the time I graduated from high school, despite all the bullying that went on, I had mastered several programming languages, learnt how to troubleshoot computer problems, and developed more efficient codes and subroutines. It was during this time in my life that I started to draw parallels between machine and human brain programming and mind coding.

It made me aware how I and everyone else around me communicated and functioned like computers; according to a set of instructions, principles, rules, beliefs and values injected by an external authority.

For those of you who may not know, computer code or program code is the set of instructions forming a computer program which is executed by a computer. It is one of two components of the software which runs on computer hardware, the other being the data.

Your brain has those two components, the hardware being the brain itself, and the software being everything the brain does with the data it has, and is continuously receiving, through the senses.

During this time, I also spent most of my weekends in my parent's garage, repairing TVs, radios and other electronic equipment that my friends and family would bring. Every time I fixed something, some of my life's questions would be answered. I understood that computers, too, were built in our image, and as a reflection of our awareness of our actual being.

I knew then, as I know now, that computers and technology, especially the development of more advanced synthetic intelligence, will amplify particular intellectual abilities of humankind; and the effects that this will have on society would far outstrip anything we had seen thus far.

Just the way computers can only execute the machine code instructions that form part of their instruction set; your brain too can only run on the mind's code instructions which are part of its instruction set.

Because these instructions are too complicated for humans to read, and because writing good programs in machine code or other low-level programming languages is a time-consuming task, many programmers like myself learn to write in the source code of a high-level programming language.

The reason this is so important to acknowledge is that your brain operates in the same way. Your mind's program is built according to the environment you live in. That includes your family, the schools you attended, the friends you hang out with, and the social and economic situation you live under.

Your brain uses old programming that was developed by others over a lifetime. However, most people's mind's programming was written at a low level of thinking. It is this low-level thinking code that was injected into your brain from a very young age that causes many people to lose control, feel afraid to make a change, and unwillingly sabotage their success in life.

As a result, you may consciously or unconsciously believe and say to yourself or others things like 'I can't do this'. 'I feel powerless'. 'If I do this, what will my parents, partner, children, friends think of me'? 'You must do as you told, otherwise God will punish you'. 'Shame on you'. 'I need to work hard to make it in life'. 'I am nobody'. 'Who am I kidding, if I have not made it in life so far there is no chance I can make it going forward'. 'I am shy'. 'I am not as good looking, smart and successful as the son or daughter of so and so'. 'My time is up'. 'The world is not safe'. 'Life is always hard'. 'People are too greedy'. 'Money does not grow on trees'. 'There are not enough resources in the world'. 'Not enough clients'. 'Not many jobs', and the list goes on and on.

Each time I faced a hardship, I would realise how damaging the outdated mind programs, codes and subroutines that had developed throughout my life were; especially in 2009, the year my job was made redundant. After being laid off, I spent a lot of time self-reflecting, studying the Law of Attraction, and gain deeper awareness on how unconscious low levels of thinking create most of the situations you and I want to avoid.

The good news is, just like computers, you too can upgrade your mind's program, and install a new mind source code that helps you process information and operate from much higher levels of awareness. Choosing to do this willingly, you can instruct your mind to execute decisions and perform tasks that will get you from where you are to where you genuinely want to be.

In parallel to my career as a senior technologist, I invested a lot of money in continuous leadership, and professional, and business development training, to help me to be the best manager I could be. This desire to know how to upgrade people's psychology most effectively led me to seek and be coached and mentored by some of the world's best leading experts in the business, personal and professional development industry.

To learn how these globally respected teachers developed their high level of thinking, I knew I had to be curious and have a high teachability index. Many of them shared how the secret to having the freedom that comes with being hugely influential and wealthy was in daily spending an hour or so to read books, develop new skills, and hire the best experts, coaches, and mentors. Every one of them, in their ways, instilled in me how by reading at least a couple of books a week, I will one day walk on the shoulders of the giants. The more I did that, the more my awareness developed in ways to make use of the power within, and the God-given wisdom of my body, mind, heart and soul.

In this commitment to upgrade my psychology, find answers to life's greatest mysteries, and travel the world to teach others to do the same, I became excellent at picking up the root cause of many of my client's problems – which I discovered was low-level language and thinking. After a consultation session with Dr. Voice's son, the former Sam Smiths vocal coach, he, like many other clients, started to call me The See-Through Coach. Each time I would hear his son use language such as 'I can't do this', I would question him until he learned to reframe his thoughts and speak in more of high-level thinking such as 'what is it I can do to make this happen.'

In computer programming, high-level languages made the process of developing a program more straightforward and more understandable, and less bound to the underlying hardware. Similarly, using high-level thinking and reframing from your language, on its own, will create visible attitude, energy, and confidence changes, which is something I am sure you are all capable of doing.

Computer language Fortran, back in 1957 was the first widely used high-level language to have a functional implementation, and many other computer languages were soon developed. In particular, Cobol aimed at commercial data processing, and Lisp specialised in computer research. Through spending late nights at my high school I understood how upgrading your psychology is nothing more than the process of designing and building an executable mind program to accomplish a specific life result.

You don't have to spend thirty years to learn all that I have, that is why I am inspired to share that information with you, through every paragraph of The Unfakeable Code®; using simple, yet useful, practical ideas and mind upgrading principles so that you can use to live authentically and freely on your own terms.

If you are a geek like me, it is most likely that you would have paid close attention to the timeline of the evolution of more sophisticated computer programming languages. You too may have realised how computer programming languages became better as more efficient codes are developed as a result of greater understanding of self, and the way our brain's work.

Similarly, your brain's (central computer) language and the programming of it (the data) has evolved in parallel with the evolution of our understanding of life, scientific breakthroughs while equally embracing our material and spiritual selves.

My lifelong quest to learn more efficient and effective ways to maximise human potential helped me to accrue the knowledge to create the scientifically proven principles you'll be reading about that I now teach others globally, on how to use to solve business problems and address personal and professional challenges.

It is sensible to re-read this book often and to use the many ideas and five principles shared in each chapter consistently; for they will help you to design efficient mind codes, build high-level of thinking, and execute crucial life and business decisions with clarity and certainty. You'll be able to process information in ways that high-level thinkers do. By doing so, you too can thrive in all the critical areas of life. You become a trusted business, effective leader, and the authentic individual everyone wants to have in life. You also can go from living an ordinary life to celebrating your extraordinary achievements, whatever they may be for you.

There is plenty of scientific evidence that proves how reading books improves your brains elasticity and efficiency. Thus, reading The Unfakeable Code® multiple times will have the same effect. It will help you to upgrade your psychology, embed the five authenticity awakening principles into your habits, and develop new mind codes that will help you to solve problems intelligently; and the better and faster you become at problem-solving, the more growth you'll experience. Integrating all I am sharing in your daily life is what will help you to take back control of the direction your life is going in. The more in control you feel on the inside, the more consciously you create the reality you want to experience on the outside.

The process of programming your mind often requires you to unlearn what you have learnt previously. You also need to input new information in your brain that will build knowledge in several different subjects of your calling. You must make sure you are consistently applying what you learn, for it is through repetition that you can create desired habits and instruct your brain to think, feel and do things differently.

Responsibilities accompanying and related to programming your mind include formal education, learning a skill, reading books, playing an instrument, art, outdoor activities, attending business and life-enhancing training programs, etc.

For those of you who want to achieve greater things in life, I highly recommend in investing in working with a life coach, a business mentor, or hire them to come into your company to develop yourself, your leader's and your employee's emotional intelligence and awareness. Promoting coaching as an empowering tool in your company as it can help you to build worker knowledge and infuse empowering values and habits. Life coaching can help you to develop a plan on how to change your low-level thoughts to high-level ones, and be more in control of your emotions and responses to inner and outer world stimuli.

Not being your true authentic self can lead to all sorts of problems. The transient persona's mask you show to the world will consistently attract issues in your life. To help you identify some of the difficulties you may experience in your life created by your transient personas, check out Picture 1. It contains the most significant transient persona pains my clients sought my advice for.

Transient Persona Pains

Business:
- Unclear Vision and Mission
- Poor Employee Engagement
- Increased Absenteeism
- Job dissatisfactions
- Poor time management
- Stress & performance issues
- Employee Conflicts
- Communication Issues
- Decline in sales
- Leadership & Retention Issues
- Fear of success, failure
- Unclear Business Strategy

Wellbeing:
- Addiction & Phobias
- Poor Mental Health
- Loss of vitality
- Loss of passion
- Physical health issues
- Anxiety, Frustrations
- Fears, Judgements
- Uncontrollable emotions

Money:
- Not Enough Money
- Spend it Easily
- Problems attracting More Worry
- Stress about wealth
- Fear of loosing Money

Career:
- Stuck in daily grind
- Boredom, Frustration
- Disillusionment
- Stress & Underpaid
- Lack of work-life balance
- Redundancy
- What to do next

Love:
- Lack of self-worthiness, self-esteem, self-confidence, self-love
- Power Games, Infidelity
- Use love as ways to control
- Co-dependency, boredom
- Communication, lies

Mental:
- Lack of clarity
- Negative self talk
- Head full of noise
- Limiting beliefs
- Not living their highest values
- OCD, Epilepsy & other mental issues

Spiritual:
- Existentialist fears
- Lack of Spiritual Connection
- Life has no meaning
- No direction
- Fear of wasting life
- Fear of death
- Fear of losing out
- Fear of judgment day
- Regrets
- Not enough spiritual

Relationships/Social Life:
- Breakup issues, divorce
- Loneliness, lack of intimacy, sex
- Pain from past relationships
- Losing a loved one
- Communication Breakdown
- Controlling Issues
- Masculine & Feminine Dynamics
- Introverted-Extroverted

Consider every chapter of The Unfakeable Code® as part of the mind's upgrading process that helps you to become aware of, dissolve and resolve any of the pains mentioned in the above picture.

Use the principles you'll be learning about intelligently; they have been proven to help you create the certainty, freedom, and fulfilment that your heart and soul is seeking. It is up to you to apply them daily to upgrade your thinking, develop conscious engineering techniques, and create best practices that will help you to enhance your mental and emotional faculties.

At times, you may need to adopt reverse engineering, an opposite process of consciously engineering your mind's programming so that you can refine your mind's code as your life's wants and needs evolve. If you let it, each page content will also teach you how to be your own mind's hacker. And, who you become as a result of hacking your mind is a choice only you can make.

It's an undeniable scientific fact that your brain is programmable. Therefore, whatever program your mind may be running in any given moment; it contains relevant and outdated codes that developed through direct experiences and centuries of evolution. So your mind's information, computing power and the memories you have grown to date, started in your mother's womb.

Some psychologists who have had a significant influence on elevating my thinking include Professor Robert B. Cialdini, whose 1984 book 'Influence: The Psychology of Persuasion' helped me to understand how persuasion can help me transform my life. Dale Carnegie's book 'How to Win Friends and Influence People' also assisted me in getting out of my mental rut making my experiences more rewarding and prosperous.

The British neuropsychologist Brenda Milner was regarded as the 'founder of neuropsychology' and the cognitive psychologist

Gordon H. Bower was noted for his 'research into memory and concept learning'. It was he who introduced the memory tool known to many life and business coaches as 'chunking'; whereby objects are grouped together in an individual's mind, to improve recall.

Above all, the words of wisdom and teachings of the following world renowned teachers and leaders: Oprah, Michelle and Barack Obama, Jack Canfield, Brian Tracey, Wayne Dyer, Barbara Brennan, Loise Hay, Tony Robbins, Deepak Chopra, Amit Goswami, Marianne Williamson, Rhonda Byrne, Warren Buffet, Robert Kiyosaki, Vishen Lakhiani, Daniel Priestly, Dr, Joe Dispenza, Steve Harrison, Nick Nanton, and Dr. John Demartini have had a profound impact in every critical area of my life. Each of them taught me something different about me, my blind spots, my capabilities, and they helped me to awaken my unfakeable sleeping giant.

I used and applied all I had learned to help my clients create the same freedom, growth, and transformation I am now very grateful to have. It is what inspired me to give birth to the #1 internationally bestselling book, 'A Path to Wisdom'. The learning and lessons that came from consulting businesses from all market sectors and coaching clients from all professions became the building blocks of the twenty-five conscious engineering principles of the TJSeMethod: ALARM® that I use globally, to empower and transform people's eight critical areas of life.

Publishing my first book, was a game-changer for me, my business, my clients, and for the millions of readers who read it. I spent half of that year travelling globally, to speak, consult and teach leaders and million-plus business owners about my five-day Vital Planning for Elevated Living Private Tuition Program, in exotic locations around the world. While spending a lot of time waiting for connecting flights, I noticed how lonely we humans have become.

Very few people would say hello, strike-up a random conversation, or even look at you. The majority of people were looking down at their phones or laptops. I noticed the same behaviour in hotels, the London underground, and in the restaurants, I would dine at. Daily, I would make sure I called my mother to check on her, as after my father passed away on 25 November 2006, she lived alone most of her time, due to the troubles she was forced to go through, to visit all of us who lived and worked in six different European countries.

The void she felt after Dad passed away, the loneliness I observed in the businesses I was asked to coach, and in the places I travelled to is what inspired me to write my next multi-award winning book, '#Loneliness – The Virus of The Modern Age'. In every page, I offered immunisation against the icy touch of loneliness, social isolation, and being so technologically connected, yet disconnected from what matters the most – our human contact, and our loving hearts.

In striving to provide more solutions to problems no human being can escape, I felt called to write a chapter in 'Fit for Purpose Leadership #3' book. Co-authored with other experts in the leadership field, the #1 Amazon bestselling book is making waves in the leadership arena. I wrote a chapter to bring about awareness about the toxic effect that burnout, pressure, and stress has on leaders' and employee's mental wellbeing.

The clearer I became about the many effects low-level thinking had on every crucial area of life, the more I wanted to write about the important role that authenticity plays in improving our businesses and our personal and professional lives. I used the 'Stay home, Save the NHS, Save Lives' government-imposed restrictions to tackle the global Coronavirus pandemic, and to write The Unfakeable Code® with a mission to share principles for leading with authenticity and living freely on your own terms.

While the deceptive strategies that your transient personas show to the world may look different in every chapter, the knowledge of the power that your unfakeable individual possesses remains constant.

Throughout history, every scholar, psychologist, scientist, philanthropist and philosopher developed knowledge, tools, and codes that allowed changes and corrections to be made to our mind's programming.

Whatever the approach to developing and upgrading your psychology and mind's codes may be, it needs to satisfy some fundamental rules. With my 'healer, gig and human behaviour specialist' hat on, that I embedded into every chapter of The Unfakeable Code®, the following five mind-upgrading, life-enhancing, and business-transforming principles are applicable:

1. To Unmask Yourself is to Know Thyself – Throughout your awakening life, you are taught to wear masks that conceal your authentic identity, masking the part of yourself that is unfakeable and limitless in its expression. To identify the self-deceptive persona's mind bug that may be causing you a problem in a running a high-level thinking program requires you to debug your mind's code. Mind debugging involves embracing traits you disown and taming the judge in you. Unmasking yourself is a vital task in the unfakeable code development process since disassociation and one-sidedness in your mind's program can have significant consequences for you. Embracing your unfakeability is good for the overall health of your body, mind, heart and soul. In this chapter, you'll come to understand how the transient masks you show to the world serve you until you are ready to face your unfakeable self, and show to the world all that you are and are not.

2. Stop Working to Survive, Wake-Up and Thrive – Your scarcity persona is causing you a problem in running a high-level thinking program. In this chapter, you'll come to understand how it is your mind's programming that stops you from having the job that you love, the business you can't wait to wake up to in the morning or having that relationship where you feel loved and nurtured. What you input into your mind determines the output, what you think, and the meaning you create. To upgrade your systems for extraordinary living, you need trust, personal responsibility, and consistency in adopting healthy behaviours, habits and values that will get you to your desired destination. By changing your language, you can achieve a particular personal, professional or business outcome. Many of you stop thriving because you become people-pleasers. Implementing the five unique ways shared at the end of this chapter will help you identify what makes you take the required actions needed for you to thrive in every area of life.

3. Disarm Your Emotional Field to Build an Impenetrable Shield – To master your emotions is to learn how to use them intelligently. In doing so, you respond objectively to anticipated problems, life situations, and confrontations. Being in control of your reactions allows you to be more in control of your mental, emotional, physical, and financial wellbeing; and, how well you act in response to an external stimuli, determines how much you repel or attract abundance, opportunities and people, in your life. In this chapter, you'll learn how having emotional mastery can help you turn crises into blessings, can tame the warrior of your emotive persona, and ultimately it can save your life.

4. Taking Back Control is an Inside Job – Letting the outside determine how you feel on the inside is what diminishes your genuine ability. In this chapter, you'll learn how by knowing your impulsive persona's behaviours, you can integrate your powerless persona into the authentic individual you know you are. Not letting your arguments convince you can help you to look within yourself to see what it is that needs healing. Use all of the five principles to go from doing to undoing, and to integrate your transient personas into being your unfakeable authentic individual. Develop a behaviour whereby, for every outer stimulus, you look within yourself for answers. The more you do this, the more you encourage your curiosity, creativity, and capability, in order to address what pains, you, lovingly.

5. Chose Love as Your Military Commander who Wins Every Battle in Life – Judgments of yourself and by others creates the resistance you feel between your mind, heart, and soul. Throughout this chapter, you'll learn how to love the unlovable in you, and to practise more kindness along with care and freedom in your interactions with yourself and others. You get to know how to dismantle the protective mechanisms of your tough love persona, heal your inner child, and diffuse conflicts in all relationships. You increase the amount of love flowing through your system, which then plays a large part in finding true love, and in solving the business, personal, professional and collective conflicts of current events and future transitional times.

At some point, you'll have to face the consequences of your choices, and most likely you'll lose everything you worked very hard to build. However, being honest in your endeavours wins the trust of the people who can get you anywhere you want. How carefully you manage your mind's resources; for example, spring cleaning your mind's one-sided psychology and memory leaks determines how trustworthy and free you can become. It also determines how well you manage the funds in your outer reality, and ultimately how much growth you can create.

Use the above five-principles of The Unfakeable Code® to help you to adopt behaviours that are best suited for the vision you want to create for your life and any task at hand. Building a mental and emotional framework that acknowledges the importance of the interconnectedness of all life plays into the kind of experiences you create in life.

When the above five principles of The Unfakeable Code® are applied in business, it signifies the following objectives:

1. Think Values first!
2. Intelligently Use and Manage Emotions!
3. Understand Human Behaviour, and its Power!
4. Put Some Heart into the Business!
5. Let Authenticity and Objectivity Shape Your Inspired Destiny!

The more you practise, repeat, and action the five principles you'll be learning more about in the following chapters, the more you will increase your chances to unlock life's miracles existing in the infinite wisdom present in all of us.

Use each principle to nurture your body, upgrade your mind's code and grow your soul. Every single rule is a guide that can turn your inner discord and chaos into outer order and success. Each chapter is written in a way that artfully and scientifically teaches you how, by being true to your authentic self, you can take back control of the direction you want your life to go; and, as Captain Jean-Luc Picard from the Star Trek Enterprise series would say, "To boldly go where no man has gone before!" To chart a precise life plan you can follow, and go from where you are to where you want to be in life.

As you read each chapter, you will awaken your God-given intelligence and inspire those around you to do the same. You'll come to understand how your low-level thinking is no longer serving you if you are aiming to live, lead and love authentically and freely. You'll realise how by embracing the ocean of wisdom that you have, the interconnectedness of all life, you can draw practical knowledge that will help you to thrive in every critical area of life.

The more you do this, the more you stimulate senses you never thought you had. You start to observe people, events, and everything internal and external with objectivity; through a new pair of lenses that spot opportunities to do greater things in life. You find ways to serve more people, to have more fun and increase your health, wealth, and wisdom. Speaking with authenticity will become more and more natural to you.

Many of your 'default' neural networks will be activated as your mind wanders from one story to another, and other dormant brain systems are activated when you answer the many quality questions that bring greater clarity into your life. Distinctly different neuro networks are activated during exercises designed for you, including the recommended guided meditations, accompanying online courses, and attending any of my talks, global seminars, or retreats.

Practising all that you'll be learning will help you see the hidden order of the role that yours and other people's masked personas play in your ever-evolving purpose in life. You'll be mystified by the new levels of awareness that became accessible to you. Achievements that once seemed impossible suddenly become possible; so will your experiences of feeling free, light, and peaceful. The expansion of your consciousness beyond the physical body will teach you many other valuable lessons.

Choosing to live with authenticity becomes the default behaviour and the lens through which you create, examine and acknowledge the presence of love in all matters, living and non-living. You slowly shift to a more favourable reality where you have the freedom to do what once you could not.

Whether or not you realise this, your experience of the world – and, thus, your behaviour – will be strongly influenced by your upgraded mind's programs. Hence the perspective you have on all that you observe will shift and change. So will your attitudes towards yourself and others. Your authentic power will start to attract people, situations and particular experiences you want to have in life.

Your unfakeable way of being will close some doors with people you once knew and open many doors with people who inspire you to attain the freedom and the transformation you are seeking, and the success you wish to skyrocket. Adopting, learning, and using each principle daily will help you to own your power, grow your worth, and lead your personal, professional, and business life, with mindful awareness.

In a sentence: The Unfakeable Code® is about fundamentally transforming how you approach every critical area of your life: spiritual, mental, emotional, physical, relationship, social, business (career and work), and wealth, so that you can freely rule in the seat of your soul's kingdom, your heart.

Let's begin.

Take Off the Mask; Your Soul is Waiting

Principle #1:
To Unmask Yourself Is to Know Thyself.

Somewhere deep inside of you, behind every masked persona you show to the world, patiently awaits your soul.

How true is that ...

Intuitively you know there's an intelligence within that equally frightens and empowers you, a resourceful intellect that guides you in every awakening moment of your physical and spiritual life. A teacher and a student patiently awaiting your instruction somewhere hidden in the kingdom of your soul, with a knowledge of something much more potent than your present moment's awareness of it.

You have a power and a knowing of what your soul's calling in life is that no one else around you can explain the way you can.

There, deep inside your heart, your mind and your soul's kingdom lies a scientist who can bring into the physical world the greatest invention ever created; a doctor who can heal your body and wounds, in a way no one else can. There, deep inside of you lies every version of you imaginable. Learning to unleash this knowledge of your authentic power is what can help you to succeed in unimaginable ways.

What if you could access this intelligence and the power it can unleash in your life, to help you not only to survive but to thrive in every area of life? How remarkable would that be?

Have you ever wondered if what you have learned so far about yourself may be 'fake news'? A statement former President Donald Trump frequently used when he is being shamed and blamed by so many media channels, and as a result, millions of us globally associate it with the president himself.

So, here's the thing, what would change in your mind if what's labelled as 'fake news' may sometimes be genuine and at other times not? To see how much of what you know about yourself may be untrue, ask yourself the following:

What would change in your awareness and your state of being if the faces of the billions of people are simply the masked representation of yourself? Would you criticise others if in the eyes of every person you meet you saw an unfakeable expression of the exact same intelligence that lives in you? Would you then be more willing to change your behaviour towards others who confront your values? Or perhaps, would you change your response towards those who have a different life ideology from the one you may be holding dear to your heart? Would you agree that if you observed others from a non-judgmental space, you would suddenly become more accepting of everyone around you? That you would feel more inner peace? That you would think you have the power to change things in your life that previously you might have thought were unchangeable?

The truth is, that throughout our awakening lives, we all wear masks that conceal our authentic identity, masking the part of ourselves that is unfakeable, authentic and limitless in its expression.

From birth, consciously or unconsciously, you are taught by others to hide your power masterfully, but at some point in your life, you are faced with the question; **for what reason and at what price do I do this?**

No matter what you do or don't do, what you say or don't say, who you love or don't love, the soul concealed behind your fake masks is always there to comfort you; to make you face the truth. Unbeknown to you, it knows the role that self-deception plays in your ever-evolving purpose in life. Your self-deceptive persona is so intelligent that it takes many forms throughout your life, and it never stops changing the mask.

It evolves with every fake persona you show to the world, and it has a unique purpose throughout your life. It can make you die, or it can help you to survive, to hide from the abusers, the bullies, the racists, the narcissists, the sadists and the many people you may come across who try to inflict you with unbearable pain. "Why would they do that?" you ask. It's because they too are living in pain.

While on the one hand self-deception may hinder your growth and cause you harm, on the other hand, the fake masks created by it are helping you to numb your temporary pain until you grow your power, your resilience and your strength. It is often said, 'What does not kill you makes you stronger'. Even if you have a physical issue, your body heals you. It evokes all sorts of chemical reactions that are necessary to fight disease, to save you and to help you heal.

Think of a moment in your life where you adopted a self-deceptive persona that made you feel safe, robust and unstoppable. It is in that moment of adversity that life throws at you for the objective of growing, that your soul's voice, hidden behind those masks if listened to, can give you the courage to overcome life's hurdles and succeed in every vital area of life.

The next time you find yourself in pain, see if you can identify what part of yourself is trying to communicate to you and for what reason. Listening to what emerges from within may help you to determine which part of your disowned persona is controlling your choices in life, that you have not loved.

You are not alone in creating what I call a 'response ready persona' hidden behind its very associated mask, we all do it, we all have them, and we all use them. As a result, we all find ourselves trying to figure out who our authentic being truly is. We have so many aspects to ourselves, and yet, despite this knowledge, the irony is that we try to 'fit' into one 'fixed persona', which becomes our momentary 'favourable' transient identity. At that moment, it is the mask we show to the world.

At some point in your life, often when disaster strikes, when the pain within becomes unbearable, you start to question the unquestionable. You begin the journey to unmasking thyself, so you can get to know and grow yourself.

It is on this journey that many of you realise how you've forgotten that within every one of us there lies a toddler who loves to be held in the arms of our loving parents. There is an inner child that loves to cry, and play in the mud, sand and water; a disobedient teenager who doesn't listen, who screams, and has no concern about getting drenched in the rain on a cold day. That there is an ambitious adult, who loves to solve problems, and enjoys spending hours daydreaming about life's most precious gifts.

There, deep within you, lies your authentic individual trying to make its mark in the world. An individual who is a student and a teacher of life, who gives altruistically and takes egotistically, and who loves to bring tears and smiles upon faces. There, somewhere hidden inside, lies a person who loves to give and receive selflessly, who at times hates and at times loves.

And yet, somehow, we fool ourselves into thinking that we are one-sided individuals who need masks to cover this very complicated definition of us, a definition that will take infinity to demystify and unmask. Why? – because we are limitless by nature, and because of the wounded persona we hold onto that needs healing, is a people pleaser, and wants to prove a point.

Have you noticed how when somebody comes and asks you who you are, you feel that you need to have an answer? but a voice within is saying: 'F**ck you, I am not interested. why would I tell a stranger about all of the persona's I am and can think of'?

Remember the last time you went on a date, a job interview, networking or met a client? Which persona did you swiftly pull out of your magician's hat and use to benefit you at that moment? Was it I am Mr. perfect or Mrs I can do it all?

Depending on the situation, whatever stage in life you find yourself in, you may either bring out the self-deceptive persona that exaggerates things about you or the one that minimises and undervalues your true abilities; or a mixture of both.

We have all met people who at times, we feel are not them at all. We label them as fake, and judge them according to our expectation of who they have to be, should be or must be. Why, because we feel we know better than them, and unbeknown to us, we are so used to injecting our values onto them that we don't even see it as a problem.

There is a part of our brain that creates the very toxic behaviour of injecting our values onto others that we automatically feel resistant towards. If you are in alignment with your authentic individual, you will acknowledge that what you observe in others also exists within you. All you have to do then is to ask yourself this powerful question: **In what form does what I judge in others show up in my life.**

In my work, I often come across people who describe themselves as introverted and sensitive, but nevertheless positive, lovely people. They would love nothing more than peace for the world, and to feel kindness and sensitivity around them.

However, when I ask them about times in their lives when they felt challenged by someone, their true authentic identity, hidden by the mask they initially chose to show, is revealed. They tell me how their sole purpose is to go to war against people who challenge their beliefs, ideology, and values. Their warrior persona comes out to vigorously defend what they believe in and value the most.

After asking them few quality questions that can demystify their perceptions of an event, they come to acknowledge how skewed perceptions can hide the truth, the love that is always there, even when challenged. At that moment, they are getting in touch with that part of their being that is extroverted, insensitive, and arrogant.

Break the Illusion of a One-sided Positive or Negative Persona

Throughout your life, you have been told to judge that which challenges your beliefs, philosophy, religion and values, and accept what supports it. It is no wonder that you are afraid to embrace the duality of your actual authentic individual. It is this illusion that sits at the root cause of inner discord, toxic behaviour, and what stimulates the amygdala's freeze, fight or flight response, which in turn inhibits your frontal cortex function of objectivity.

In a safe space, using a combination of the TJSeMethod® and The Unfakeable Code® principles you are learning, the Demartini Method® and other transformational tools I've learned and created over the last 30 years, I assist clients in creating life-changing breakthroughs revealing to them the role their masked persona plays in their ever-evolving life. Through carefully designed questions and exercises they learn to establish an inner equilibrium and create business, professional and personal breakthroughs.

Using what you are learning in every chapter of this book can help you to do the same. You can use them all. I am teaching you to diffuse emotional charges that silently destroy your physical, mental, and emotional being.

In your unfakeable authentic reality, nothing is missing, but in your transient persona reality, you tend to think everything is missing and you keep giving in to your one-sided perceptions. Your ability to see the unseen is what helps you to acknowledge both sides of the meaning you've attached to a specific event. You come to accept the role that your self-deceptive persona plays in your one-sidedness. It is this recognition that helps you to create long-lasting breakthroughs.

In seeing through the messages that the judgement of others brings to your awareness, you too can start to develop the mindset needed to own the traits that you either like or despise in others. The more you do that, the closer you get to your real authentic being, the more radiant you become. Thus, it is wise to invest your energy, money and time in a qualified coach, mentor, or facilitator, to help you to go through this breakthrough process safely.

Invest all you have into all you want to create is the advice I give to everyone who seeks growth, fulfilment and transformation; because I know from personal experience that it pays off in the long run. It is also why many successful people you may know and many of my global clients have invested in being unfakeable; to assist them to awaken their authentic leader, grow their power and give rise to a radiant individual who is grateful, inspired, and unstoppable.

In challenging these one-sided perceptions of the various transient personas emerging from the countless masks, you too can reveal those parts of yourself that you have abandoned, disowned and are calling you to love. Next time you admire an energetic, extroverted, tough individual who can handle anything that comes his or her way, remember that they too have vulnerabilities. They may also have a weak, introverted, soft persona inside them who is afraid, drained of his life force and at times feels helpless.

Your job is to break the illusion created by the exterior façade you and everyone around you shows to the world. You can do so by listening to the voice of your genuine, authentic and unfakeable being who knows when you are lying and will keep reminding you that it is your self-deceptive nature that misleads you.

The next time you find yourself in moments of hardship, one of the things you can do is to remember times when you felt so powerful, how, like a volcano, your authentic power emerged from within you. Give it a go, and let your powerful intellect help you to strengthen your confidence, intuition and will.

Sometimes, you might find yourself in situations or with people who waste most of your energy by pretending on the outside to be someone you feel they are not, on the inside. The more you do this as a way to please others, the further apart you will be from your true authentic identity. This inner conflict is also the root cause of your pain, shame, guilt, and the reason why you will find it hard to overcome hardships, get back on track and happily live in the flow of life.

From a very young age, I was fascinated with the masks people wore in my family, in the local community, and even in the black and white films I had once spent hours watching. As an adult, I admired people's creativity in creating every possible mask one could think of and wearing them in various carnivals held around the world. Don't forget, I may feel as young as you, although I was born in the winter of 1969 and in the '70s and my childhood reality was shaped by James Dean, Charlie Chaplin, Marylin Monroe and Brigitte Bardot.

In 1999, the year after I graduated, I first attended The Carnival of Venice, world-famous for its elaborate masks, gondolas and breath-taking architecture. I remember wearing a costume I bought from a local store and asking myself the questions:

Why do people hide behind the masks called nationality, creed, profession, religion, wealth, etc.? Why are the masks we wear every day generally used as an excuse for arguments, division, occupation and war? Why don't we use them like the people in the Carnival of Venice do, which is to celebrate diversity and dance in unity with the rhythm of life?

Truth be told, back then, at twenty-nine years old, having survived the atrocities of the civil war, I did all I could to get my life back on track. I did three jobs to pay for my full-time electrical engineering and management studies degree at University College London, and I made sure that I would graduate from one of the top universities in the UK.

To safeguard myself from predators, I lived daily being a people pleaser, hiding my pain, and who deep down, I knew I was. I did all I could to stay away from folks who in my presence, would always throw around xenophobic and hateful remarks about migrants, refugees, and people of different ethnic and religious backgrounds. Each time there was a societal problem, many newspapers would blame migrants, yet they would never mention the positive role migrant models who, like myself, had worked 18 hours a day in jobs not many British people would even contemplate doing.

My frightened penniless being, with no family to turn to for love, help and protection, had to survive somehow. I managed to calm my mind by working long hours, studying late at night, meditating and having on average three to four hours sleep per night. I became excellent at finding ways to fit into a new city that, after the atrocities of the civil war, had become a safe sanctuary and a home for me and for many others like me.

Hidden from my awareness, my identity crisis and inner conflicts gave power to my ever-evolving self-deceptive persona. Whether I liked it or not, I learnt how to blend into environments that felt unsafe, including being around some friends and family members. The fear of not being good enough, being rejected or being killed for being different from others engulfed my day to day life. To survive, I would put on a brave mask and I would make sure that very few people knew, who I was inside.

We all find ourselves going through moments in our lives when we don't know who we are. When we feel that there is nothing left to live for, when, from fear of judgment and rejection, we don't show our actual personality and feelings to others; but, we also have moments in our lives when we dare to be all that we can be.

Usually, for many of us, those moments where we show our unfakeability when there is no one around us to see and judge our vulnerabilities. Our self-deceptive nature is what makes us fill the inner voids with uncontrollable drinking, indulging ourselves at a bar or a night club where no one knows us.

For twenty-years, in parallel to my career as an engineer and information technology manager, I spent a lot of energy, time and money on trying to 'fix' my broken self and fill the voids that had a mind of their own. I studied long hours, researched and bought the best self-development tools, learned about Neuro-Linguistic Programming, Cognitive Behaviour Therapy, the Sedona Method, The Demartini Method, Neuroscience, Quantum Physics, and I trained as a qualified transformational life coach, firstly to help myself.

The more I transformed my life, the more I wanted to assist others with what I had learnt in overcoming challenges to overcome challenges presented to them in any of the crucial areas of their lives. It was while I was on this journey that I was called to dedicate my life's work to understanding the complexities of human behaviour, the body-mind-soul relationship, and our material and spiritual essence, to work for the benefit of humankind.

The more I learnt, the more my desire to teach others how to unleash the freedom in their potential grew. My childhood dream to write books, travel the world to speak and to teach others what I was learning became a reality that I now found myself in. I realised that everything I had learnt had prepared me for this moment, and to continuously take inspired action steps to fulfil my heart's calling; which is to ignite the God-given intelligence in the hearts of a Billion People.

The more I learned about engineering, technology, management, human behaviour, Eastern methods of healing, physiology, psychology, biology and sociology, the more I became aware of how we as humankind use masks to conceal the power and the strength of the unfakeable identity present in all of us.

On my birthday December the 12th 2013, after meditating for a few hours on a decision I had to make, the course of my life changed forever and for the better. I saw the exact reason why our imaginary, transient personas, and the masks we show to the world play in our ever-evolving purpose in life.

They were there to protect us until the moment we unleashed the power within, and could authentically and safely channel the infinite God-given energy for our benefit and for the benefit of all humankind. I learnt how, in those moments, when we are ready to face the truth of who we indeed are, that we grow the most.

This inspired me to share my realisations through writing books, and teaching globally everything I had learnt to first and foremost help people harmonise the relationship between their inner demons and angels. The more at peace you become with those two powerful forces within you, the more you start to unleash the freedom and the power that lives in your authentic, and unfakeable individual self.

In your heart, you know that this power you possess isn't given to you by whatever creator you believe in, merely to be hidden, misused, and put aside! It is provided to you to be all you can be, to become masterful in navigating your journey to your desired consciously created destiny.

The more entrepreneurs, business owners, CEO's and people from all professional backgrounds I taught how to channel this authentic power safely and wisely, the more confident they felt; and the more grounded, successful and masterful they were becoming. I started to see the evidence I was seeking that showed how, in swiftly transforming their transient masks, they would live, love, and lead more authentically. In some cases, if they did not do or continue to do the work, their self-deceptive persona would evolve into an even more egotistical, power-hungry persona.

Just like some of my clients who stopped learning, you too, if you're not careful, your own false persona's voice may create the illusion that you know it all. The more you use what you are learning to be playful with observing yourself and taking off the mask that no longer serves you, the more you start to see the presence of something beautiful and powerful that is guiding and transforming you from within.

However, don't be fooled, your self-deceptive nature can also use the same power to feed the one-sided ego persona that can take you to the opposite side of being a self-destructive, bipolar, OCD, infatuated and narcissist persona. I know in my heart, that if you apply everything you are reading throughout the book, answer every question asked, and embody the wisdom of every story told, it will safely guide you on the journey to share with the world your unfakeable identity openly.

It is up to you to commit to a lifelong process and make it your intention to learn how to unmask yourself so that you can live more of an authentic life; so that life can then expose itself authentically to you.

Change the Thoughts You Think, Words You Speak and the Language You Use

Leonardo da Vinci once said, "Fire is to represent truth because it destroys all sophistry and lies and the mask is for lying and falsehood, which conceals the truth." This fable is as relevant now as it was when he wrote it. So is Victor Marie Hugo's quote, a French poet, novelist, and one of the greatest and best-known writers who once said, **"Virtue has a veil, vice a mask."**

Think and meditate long enough on the above quotes and every word I am sharing for they'll help you awaken the power the words carry and the intelligence residing in your heart's knowing. In doing so, you'll start to observe a divine order in all that you experience. You will become more at ease with embracing the duality of your nature, loving who you are in your essence, and authentically sharing your being with the world.

Don't forget, that from an early age, the process of developing the many façades of your varied personas to show to the world begins. Many of you, were injected with the values of various authority figures, that were designed to make you conform to external definitions of who and what you are, should be, and according to some people, must be. With the passing of time, you forget that behind all of your façades built from conformity and disassociation from your actual being, somewhere within you, there still resides your authentic soul, the very thing that makes you move, powerful and unfakeable.

Like it or not, you learn to worry about your physical appearances, you become fearful of how others perceive you, and you put on a temporary mask. You forget to love yourself as you are, and for who you are. You become a chameleon to survive, yet you ignore the hero within and its ability to help you thrive.

Instead of consciously creating your dream life, you unconsciously bring about the feeling of spiritual death, of feeling directionless and not knowing your purpose in life. You learn to falsely observe life using filters that conceal your real identity. In doing so, you experience life through the lens of the sophisticated pain management mechanisms stored behind many of the façades created by the masks of your wounded personas.

Sometimes, when I work with clients, the first thing I help them do is to become aware of how some of those protective mechanisms may have developed. In some cases, I've seen how specific emotional responses my clients experience go back to the time when they were still in the womb.

While some of you may have learned to acknowledge the self-deception of the masks you chose to wear in specific moments in your life, many of you picked up this book because you may still find it difficult to first and foremost, become aware of your masks existence and origins and how they functioned at other moments in your life.

You are reading this book because you are ready to master your life, create the success you want and to live life on your terms through being more authentic. Your curiosity, coupled with your intuition, is what is helping you to reveal your unfakeable self and the truth of who you are. Use them as you read the book. They'll help you to learn more about the transient masks you wear, and about what part of your persona created them, for what purpose, and how to change them.

Ask yourself this question: What stops me from unleashing the freedom and the power of my true authentic self?

Don't be fooled; you are not alone in asking this question. Every one of us wears masks that have many façades that we chose to show to the people we meet and to the outside world. Some of our covers may be there to deceive and falsify others and ourselves deliberately. But the majority of the façades most of us have, are created by parts of our being that judge our intrinsic qualities and traits.

The masks that your transient personas wear have as much power over you as the choices and decisions you make that are based upon injected values that come from a perceived authority. The more choices and decisions you make, based on those inserted values, the more you feel separated from the authentic individual you were born to be. As a result, you get used to labelling and judging yourself as weak, shy, uncertain, evil, greedy, narcissistic, selfish, arrogant, etc. You get the point.

From time to time, you may find yourself in situations where you have to pretend. It is in those moments that you feel you have to put on a mask and smile. Yet, deep down, you want to cry, escape and scream. You do this because at that moment you want something that supports what you value, but you don't want the pain you have not found the words to describe yet to interfere with the expected outcome. At that moment, deep inside yourself, you know you are unhappy, lonely and sad, yet you put on the mask of a happy persona to get what you want from that person or situation. You deliver what is expected of you. It is in those moments that putting on a mask helps you cover your vulnerability and temporarily supports you getting what you want. You are getting short term gain and creating long term pain.

Have you ever wondered how the façade created by the transient masked persona you show to the world may be there to reveal something about you that satisfies your deep longing to be loved, liked, and accepted?

What would you change in your life if you chose not to disguise what is emerging from you at that moment when you make unwanted choices to get what you want? Another question I often ask my clients when we work in demystifying a multitude of personas that hide our authentic self is this: "Do you want to be loved for all that you are or for the masked persona showing up at moments of need?" The answer my clients and people I meet always give me is the same, "Tony, I want to stand in my real authentic power and be loved for all that I am."

One of the things you may want to consider right now is to identify in whose presence the specific masks you put on become the weakest and the strongest influences on you. Open a word document, or take a notebook and write down their names. Ask yourself why that happens with that person or persons and what it is about them that triggers changes within you. Identify the parts of you that hurt, why that is so and what traits you are disowning that scream for your love.

There may be times in your life when you catch yourself wondering how people would react if you were to expose your true self. How about right now, is there someone in your life that deep inside, you wish to reveal your true self to? What action would you need to take? What fears will you overcome? What blessings would this bring into your life?

Your answers will guide and teach you how to embrace your real authentic self, unleash its power and thrive in life by being the unfakeable you. You will learn to be more aware of other people's masks and the role their transient identities play in theirs and your ever-evolving purpose in life.

The more unfakeable you become, the more authentic the people around you are. The more people are drawn towards you, the more they want to hire and collaborate with you. Opportunities start to emerge from nowhere. You attract the perfect clients, business opportunities, and a relationship you want to stay in. You begin to live life being more fulfilled, acknowledged and successful.

No matter who you are – an elderly person, a young adult, a professional coach, a therapist, a lawyer, a banker, a CEO, a millionaire, a billionaire, or you are merely curious and inexperienced at heart; now or at some point in your life, you will know how, deep down, that behind the illusion created by the masks you wear, awaits your soul's love, truth and wisdom.

Despite the many situations you have overcome, when the next cycle of growth happens, it will bring with it a new form of the same challenges you once thought you had overcome and mastered; being the feeling of abandonment, being a failure, being cheated, being misunderstood, being rejected, being uncared for, and so on. Or it will bring you a sense of success, acceptance, and the knowledge that you could do what was required, how to go about the task, and that you know how to overcome the obstacles.

Let's be honest here; going through times in your life when your values are challenged is hard. Once again, you will find it hard to be yourself in the presence of another authentic individual. Pay attention to this, because, if you don't, your self-deceptive nature will learn more innovative ways to falsify your true identity and stop you from expressing what you genuinely feel inside about yourself.

This was the case with John, a successful CEO working in one of the top asset management companies in New York. After my name was mentioned at a party he attended, he got in touch with me to book a consultation to help him overcome alcohol, smoking and recreational drug addictions. He asked me to help him to get his life back on track, increase his focus, improve his performance, and create a healthier work-life balance.

At the beginning of our journey, I remember how challenged he felt each time I would question him about the things he did not want to talk about. Despite spending a lot of money to help him create a breakthrough and save his job and relationship, he kept making the same excuses that got him into the place of pain where he was in his life in the first place.

He said, "Tony, I hired you because I knew that you would help me to create the breakthroughs I am seeking, and to teach me how to hold myself accountable for the excuses I come up with." In every session, he would share a story that he felt charged about, and I would get him to take notes of the answers he came up with to the questions I asked. Together we would identify the specific traits he disowned and was being charged about.

When we looked at how some of the behaviours that conflicted with the values he upheld so highly had served him, we got to the bottom of his anger, fears and judgments of himself that were the root causes of many of his addictions. A year later, having neutralised many of his emotional issues, he admitted to me that at the end of our first session, he had felt there was a 'killer' persona inside him that wanted to harm me or anyone else who did not agree with him.

Whether you acknowledge it or not, this self-destructive 'killer persona' exists in you and in all of us, and it is an amygdala triggered reaction – The amygdala is the part of the brain that regulates your 'fight', 'freeze' or 'flight' response. If when your values are challenged, you perceive that the threat is too significant to handle, you feel that you are the pray, and you chose to fly. If you recognise the person who is challenging your values as weak, your reptilian brain see him or her as prey, and you fight. Or, alternatively, you may freeze at that moment.

As we continued to work together, John clarified what was most important to him. He had learnt the importance of seeing the benefits and the drawbacks of the many beliefs, behaviours, values or traits he either liked or disliked. The more we did this, the more authentic he became, the more productive he was in the boardroom and the more energy he had in the bedroom. He started to have a healthy sex life again and he re-ignited his love for his wife.

The more I taught him how to see all he was experiencing through an objectivity lens, by examining both sides of the many disowned traits hidden behind the masks, the more clear-headed he became, and his confidence to tackle more significant challenges at his workplace increased. His performance, productivity, and achievements skyrocketed. Why? because the more authentic you become, the more you let go of what is weighing you down the more you embrace what makes you fly. You start to illuminate others with your authentic insights, power and wisdom.

All you have to do is to observe the kind of masks you and others wear and what reasons do you have for not going out and meeting people. Start a conversation with random strangers, talk to friends and family members, and attend networking events. You will see the difference it will make in yours and other people's lives if you listening to conversations with a non-judgmental attitude.

You may be greeted with an aggressive manner by some people, who show closed body language and looks and relay hostile intentions towards you. Your body will also feel the negative energy radiating from the masked, wounded persona who at that moment is communicating with you.

If this happens, remember that there is an authentic persona present in them too. Use the concepts shared in this book to connect to their authentic self, in terms of what they value the most. Don't forget that every one of those people you may have met, is just like you. They will use a certain mask to identify themselves at certain moments. If you met them in another moment, where your values are more aligned with each other, let's say for example, at a charity you both support, and you ask the very same questions, you will find that the new persona they exhibit who is more co-operative and willing to share, has emerged.

Every thinkable label known to humankind, such as being a doctor, social worker, waiter, scientist, philosopher, entrepreneur, gay man, straight man, coach, mentor, teacher, mother, father, prime minister, HRH the Queen, a celebrity, is nothing more than a transient persona identity that serves you until you are ready to face the truth being your unfakeable individual self.

Like me, you may have gone through times in your life when you wore the mask of an ashamed, unemployed, or helpless redundant person. Some of you may be going through a career change or a redundancy right now. Some of you may be going through times of transitioning into becoming an entrepreneur, a business owner, or a social media influencer. Don't forget that deep within you lies an immense power of an intelligence that created all those identities, just waiting to express their desires.

Unbeknown to you, it is these transient masks that conceal the truth of how powerful you really are. It is these masks you wear daily that can either create walls that imprison your authentic power or they can unleash your power and set it free.

Everything that you have not loved about your authentic being is what plants the seeds of what the society commonly labels as 'a form of mental illness'. The further away you are from the awareness of your true authentic nature, the more segregation you feel between yourself and others. If you pay attention, you will observe in your language and in other people's language phrases like 'I have to', 'you have to', 'they have to', 'must-do', 'should too'.

Thoughts are energy and so are the words you use and the sentences you construct. The further you are from inner equilibrium, the more you increase the chances of being labelled bipolar, ADHD, OCD and having some kind of mental health or emotionally associated disease. The more time you spend being unhealthy, feeling trapped and isolated, the deeper you go into the caves of the wretched solitude I talk about in the multi-award-winning book #Loneliness – The Virus of the Modern Age.

The next time you feel attacked, unsafe and misunderstood, try and spend some time to identify the behaviours, traits and the values that challenge you the most. The people who you think may make you feel this way are the same people who could bring your awareness of why you behave and respond the way you do, to you – learning to communicate with others in terms of what is important to them and lovingly, is the key to your long term success. Each time you talk in terms of other people's values, you will feel more appreciated, loved and more likely to be asked to consult or do business with them.

I will forever be grateful to all of my teachers and mentors for the clarity, love and wisdom they shared with me; especially, I would like to thank Dr John Demartini, whose clarity of teachings helped me see the hidden order and intelligence that lies in me and in every human being. On this journey with John as my mentor, I became even more inspired and confident of my journey. On many occasions, John would say to me, "Tony, you are well on your way, in your journey towards standing on the shoulders of the giants. Keep learning and keep serving more people."

His words inspired me to keep studying, to keep helping people, to keep writing and creating more efficient tools and methods that people can use to accelerate their learning, unleash their authentic power, and maximise their human potential. Incorporating all I was learning opened my path to globally help clients to be the best version of themselves in all the critical areas of life. In choosing to be the best version of ourselves, we can learn how to serve humankind by being our unfakeable authentic best selves.

There are many models of knowing your values, the one I use the most with my clients and I am certified for is the Demartini Value Determination Process®. As a business coach who specialises in human awareness, behaviours that drive fulfilment and peak performance; before I start on any significant business or leadership consultation work with my clients, I first establish their need. I then explain with educational and fun metaphors the problems they are experiencing and what they are doing right and what they should work at to change.

Before we do any further work, I determine their values and I help them to create, or to re-write an inspiring vision for themselves and their business that encompasses the values they hold dear in their hearts. In clarifying personal and company-wide values, I then take them on an inside-out, revealing and transforming journey. I use the five-business and behaviour changing principles of The Unfakeable Code® to assess and address current challenges and then create an actionable plan that delivers clear outcomes and the results they seek.

In assisting my clients in creating a clear vision, mission, and purpose, they are then able to put together a step by step plan that they can follow through on. In showing them how to use the five-principles to empower all of the employee critical areas of life: spiritual, mental, physical, emotional, relationship, financial, business, and social, some of my clients have increased their salaries or grew their firms more than five times in less than twelve months.

Learning the difference between injected and authentic values, and consistently using the principles to upgrade your mind's code can save you years of living in pain and being unfulfilled and unproductive at work. In knowing and accepting that your mind is programmable, you start to give yourself permission to embrace who you indeed are, which is the synthesis of all the masked personas you see in the world, and every trait you know of.

What stops you seeing through the façades your self-deceptive persona shows to the world is the intensity of the fear, pain, shame and discord you experience within yourself. That is because your self-deceptive nature doesn't want you to go at that moment when you perceive that you only felt the true extent of your pain when you acknowledged the pleasure you received.

If you are someone who is either resisting or who finds it hard to acknowledge the pleasure in that moment of pain, let me ask you this; Can you have a stable atom without the balanced energy of the neutron, electron and positron? No, you can't, neither can you have experiences in life that do not have the pain, the pleasure and the transcendent associated state, which is love. Thus, it is love that can help you to glue all the transient personas into one authentic individual who is powerful beyond imagination.

When you are living in denial of the balanced presence of those three mental perceptual states, the negative emotion, the positive emotion, and love; you need to realise

that the intuitive feeling in every experience in life is what keeps you disempowered, in a state of judgment, and that is what is preventing you from recognizing in yourself what you observe in others.

When you felt fearful, that you were being judged, and criticised, you naturally put your defences high to protect yourself from feeling hurt and being attacked. Equally, when you feel acknowledged, loved, and safe in the presence of others, you unleash the power of your true authentic self. This typically happens when you are in the presence of other people who are on their journey to self-mastery.

Recently, I was hired by the CEO of a company that sells insurance policies to train their sales team. I spent the morning identifying what they did well, what hurdles they felt they couldn't overcome, and what growth they wanted to create. I knew that in using the principles, you are learning about that they would be able to identify the necessary changes needed that would give their sales team the boost that they asked me to provide.

At first, many of the sales team were doubtful about how the five-principle process could help them reach their targets and communicate better with each other. As the afternoon went on, having clarity on what their values were and teaching them how to ask each other questions that supported their values, they saw how much easier it had become to collaborate and sell to one other.

Furthermore, I showed them how, by changing the language their sales team used when emailing or phoning their prospective clients, they could get them to reveal what they truly wanted and the deep down value they sought. They put this to the test for a week, and instantly they saw how their sales grew. In knowing how to link the specific insurance product they were selling with what the customer valued the most, and the benefits it would bring to their lives, they changed their communication and sales pitch in a way that the people they cared for and loved appreciated.

After a month I went back to do another sales training immersion day, I spent the afternoon listening to how everyone used the principles and all the ideas I shared to listen better to what their customers' wants and needs were; how it enabled them to close on existing leads, achieve their sales targets and encourage happy customers to refer their products and services to their friends and family, thus creating a quadruple win, win, win, win situation.

Whether you are a solopreneur or a business, it is in your interest to learn how to communicate in the language of your client's values, and that approach will help you to disarm their self-defence mechanism, and they will then be more willing to collaborate with you and buy from you.

Communicating in terms of what is important to others is what can help you to create harmonious and long-lasting connections with others. It is through this way of identifying what other people want and communicating in terms of what they value that you become loved for who you are, for what you stand for, and for what you believe in, without the need to justify yourself. You can use this life-changing philosophy to transform your relationship with your partner, parents, children, friends, colleagues, customers, clients and so on.

John Bowlby, a British psychiatrist ahead of his time and originator of the attachment theory, stated that, "We are born with this need to have safe connections and we take this need with us "from the cradle to the grave." Only recently in the field of psychology has it become more accepted that children not only need a safe connection with others, but that every adult needs that as well, so as to be authentic, healthy, happy, content and prosperous in their lives.

The thoughts you think, the language you speak and the daily choices you make have the power to either strengthen these false façades or break them down, so unveiling your true authentic self is a choice you can make. It is through every decision that you make that you either unscrew the screws that hold the mask tightly onto your face, or you tighten them even more.

If for example, you meet someone, and if you feel some kind of resistance towards them, like it or not, your mind becomes exceptionally creative in the way it ends up judging them. You try to make sense of their reality using your values, beliefs and associated perceptions, and you pass on a 'learned criticism'. In behaving this way, you don't look within to find the answers to what creates this resistance. Instead, you waste your energy trying to change external factors you have no power to change. As you become better at recognizing the self-deceptive mechanisms of your façades, the depth of insights you get can remove the judgments and criticism you have towards others immediately.

Your approach becomes that of a non-judgmental observer of yourself and others.

Imagine for a second, the inner peace you would be living in and the deep, meaningful connections you would be making with one another through adopting a non-judgmental observation of one another. This is the place where 'I love you' and 'thank you' become an ingrained habit and response towards those who challenge you the most.

As you learn to make choices and decisions that come from an awareness of multi-sensory perception and a non-judgmental state, you start to use your emotions intelligently. It is from this harmonious place within yourself that you have the power to change your response to an external stimulus consciously.

In choosing to engage with others through your non-judgmental observer, your authentic power is unleashed from the seat of your soul, your heart. As you learn to observe reality through a multi-sensory perception, your quality of life improves. You start to trust your unfakeable self, and it's infinite abilities, wisdom and love.

In masterfully taking off your transient masks, you begin to use more of your innate skills to lift others. You create an unbreakable bond with other human beings in a much more meaningful and more profound way.

Every time my clients learn to master the process of removing the masks created by disassociation, fear and pain, I observe a noticeable difference in their aura (human energy field), behaviours, and language. Addressing new challenges that life throws at them **becomes less painful and more playful**. The more they learn how to live in alignment with their true authentic self, the easier it becomes for them to embrace their authentic power. The clarity that emerges from within gives them the confidence to express their highest version and vision of themselves.

Often at the end of a consultation, I am asked, "Tony how long or how often do you recommend for me to book sessions with you?" My response goes something like this, "How far in life do you want to go? How wide do you want your reach to be? How much of an impact do you want to make in the world? How fulfilled are you called to be?" Before I have the chance to ask another question, many of the clients who are ready to skyrocket their growth in whatever they want the most say, "I get the point, when can we start?"

If you find yourself in pain and struggling, perhaps that is the best time to look at the role this kind of mask you are showing to the world is playing in your life. Often, when I help clients to get a work promotion, I ask them this question, "What benefits are you getting in staying in your current role?" Their default response would be none, but upon further questioning, hidden motives start to surface; bringing with them perceived hidden benefits and their unconscious thinking that they would experience more problems if they got the promotion they wanted.

If you don't take on the challenge to reveal your authentic self, you will continue to create many more lopsided perceptions that fuel emotions that damage every aspect of your life.

In prolonging the process of unveiling what fear, pain or shame your masks conceal, you give power to whatever is hidden behind it. You give strength to the self-deceptive persona that segregates and falsely safeguards you in your self-made psychological prison.

With time passing the walls of this self-made prison becomes thicker, and hides from your awareness the masked persona that you show to the world. You may believe that in strengthening those walls you are protecting yourself from the perceived threat coming from your outer reality; but, your soul, patiently awaiting behind all of the masks, knows the truth; it knows it is an illusion. It is these elusive mind walls that keep you to feel insecure and insignificant. Those walls truly make you feel small and they isolate your authentic power from the rest of the world. They can stop you from living life on your terms.

Be aware; transient façades can hide the unconscious intentions of each of the disempowered personas that live within you. Your fake identity uses them as a vehicle through which it makes itself seem wiser, more experienced, more fun, more vivacious, more trustworthy, more honest than you are.

Equally, some of you may have noticed how at times when you feel uncertain about yourself you use masks as pretences so that you do not let people know how small, unworthy and vulnerable you perceive yourself to be. How critical, judgmental, fearful, angry, clueless, and susceptible deep down you feel you are. In a way, it is protecting you from self-destructing.

As daily life distractions take over, before you know it, you start to overlook the fact that it was you who built these deceptive façades in the first place. Each time you feel fearful, judged, not being good enough, being rejected and not listened to, you put on a mask, to protect yourself.

The more covers you wear that conceal your true authentic self, the harder it becomes, later on in life to recognize their presence in yourself and others. The journey to uncovering them becomes a huge hurdle to overcome, often manifesting as forms of addictive behaviours, depression, and in the worst cases, a physical or emotional illness.

Know What Truly Stops You from Taking Off your Illusory Masks

Over time, the same fear that created the illusion you may find yourself living in, the fear of looking within for answers, if not addressed, becomes more significant than the fear of the freedom awaiting you in your outer experience of life. In those moments of doubt, you can recall how your authentic self knows of the liberty in which your spirit thrives. Make sure you go within and tune into the awareness of the interconnectedness of all life, and your love for all life. This will help you feel more confident about making necessary changes in your life.

Self-deception is not just something that builds false façades of your transient persona. It is also what can help you, in your essence, to know who you are. Self-deception impacts every aspect of your being, including the value of your inner self and the outer value that people measure you by. Self-deception is a global issue that toxically affects your physical, mental and emotional being. It also impacts how good, impactful, productive and profitable an organisation is.

On one of my trips to LA, I came across the cover of an American Psychological Association's Monitor on Psychology Magazine that read 'Friends Wanted'.

This truly highlights the large and growing body of research in psychology that increasingly shows the grave health risks that self-isolation and self-deception pose to us. The effects are not just in our day to day life but also spread into every sphere of life.

Feeding your mind with negative thoughts and skewed perceptions that give rise to disempowering beliefs can lead you to instruct your subconscious mind to execute a self-destruct command. Can you imagine the impact this creates in every aspect of your life? Now imagine the impact millions of people going to work with a self-destructive program running through their mind would have on every layer of our society?

Wearing fake masks to conceal our true identity is also the thing that fuels the ever-increasing amount of world issues such as wars, environmental disasters, increase in divorce rates, suicide rates, sexual assaults, addictions, people living with depression, anxiety, and so on, that are present in every layer of society.

Giving in to your illusive masks' demands can make you desperate to be perfect, to be better than others, and to expect more and more from yourself, others, and from life itself. This need, driven by the disintegrated persona, forces you to make choices from a place of desperation and neediness. Forgetting that this way of being has a domino effect, that leads to the further disintegration of your authentic self, segregation from others, and invokes a feeling of being lonely and emotionally unstable.

The more you give power to fake personas, the more you end up in a desperate place in which your partners in crime become your addictions, fears and judgments. Alcohol, drugs, sex, gambling, sugar, video games, movies, and shopping addictions are usually just the results from a bigger problem that was not addressed in time.

At some point in life, you may have felt anxious, depressed and isolated. If so, you do know how feeling this way easily ripples into all of the eight critical areas of your life and impacts your spiritual, your mental, your emotional, your physical, your relationships, your business, your career, and your social life.

Pay attention, as your self-deceptive persona, hidden from your conscious awareness, may still be present in any of these critical areas of life, ensuring that you sabotage your success. It's typically present where you feel defeated, and it is in those areas that it thrives the most. The more critical of yourself and others you are, the less accepting of your actual authentic being you become. To be aware of this, you can pay attention to people who cause you the most pain. These people are the mirror version of the unloved part of your being, which is trying to communicate to you about your inner discord, anxiety, and rejection, instead of wanting to be loved and healed.

However, the truth is, that you can never escape facing your reality, your intuition, and the spirit that awaits you behind all the transient masks. Throughout your life, that spirit continually makes you aware of the inbuilt ALARM that alerts you when you are not in alignment with your true authentic self. It brings on people and situations that can help you heal the pain and assist others in improving their true selves.

Investing your time, energy and money to learn how to take off the masks safely and face your true authentic self is the best gift you can give to yourself; and it never loses its value.

Choosing to do nothing, is to continue to hide your true authentic self from the world and live fearfully in the shadow of your own making.

When a significant disconnection exists between your outward identity and your true authentic self, you experience an identity crisis. Your desire for freedom from pain may either lead you to seek relief by drinking alcohol, doing drugs or engaging in other toxic behaviours that may permanently damage your unfakeable self.

We spend our lives wearing different masks, and it is no wonder that most of the time, we do not even know how to distinguish the masked persona from the real authentic individual that is as unique as your fingerprint or your retinal identity.

The more differences you observe in others, the more masks you wear, the deeper you hide your true authentic self. Learning how to use the authentic principles you share will assist you in becoming better at observing life and people from a balanced perspective, and the weaker the power of the masks you use to cover up parts of yourself that you don't like will become; and, the less desire you will have to change how people perceive you.

The mask you are wearing is the reason that causes many of you to detach from the connection you have with one another. It is why so many people instead of looking within, judge one another, and ultimately they give power to their self-deceptive one-sided illusion of self. A famous quote that I often use when I am invited to deliver a keynote speech or inspire an audience says, "You are only ever loved to the extent that you are vulnerable, honest and truthful".

You cannot feel loved for who you are as long as you are not known as you truly are.

The irony is, that at the same time, if you want to remove your mask, your self-deceptive nature fears you exposing your true self. It makes you think that you will be rejected, unloved, and uncared for if you do so.

This frustrating self-deceptive cycle is what I observed happening at various stages in my clients, and many of the people's lives I come across in my day to day work. It is this fear of being seen for who you are that keeps your authentic self-imprisoned behind your masks, and hence, your relationships become shallow, unfulfilling, and uncaring.

In today's culture of 'keeping up with the Kardashians', it is no surprise that most of you find yourself stuck living a fake life in a virtual world that can eat up your most precious possession, your time. You feel trapped in a never-ending rat race of living up to what you think other people expect of you. Your moods end up being regulated by another masked persona seeking validation. Meanwhile, your authentic individual is left to choke itself in the dust left behind by the sandstorms created by your fake persona, unheard and craving for your attention.

As a human being, you have a natural desire to grow, change and progress, but, because of your transient persona's need to please others, too often the motivation for change is external, rather than driven by your authentic highest values, intuition and your soul's knowing. You know that this type of externally motivated change never lasts. With time, you end up feeling frustrated and often you find yourself back at square one. I see many people who are driven by outside motivation eventually meet with inner feelings of abandonment, disappointment and unworthiness; not to mention a sense of being uncared for and unloved.

Let's face it; life will always have its ups and downs; what I am sharing with you in this and in the following chapters is a way of living, a way of thinking and **a proven blueprint to being**

unfakeable. As you learn to remove the elusive masks that conceal the uniqueness which lies within you, you will start to live, love and lead every aspect of your life with authenticity. The things that you hide about yourself are the very things that can unleash your authentic power and put you on a path to living and leading with excellence.

Unloved parts of you play a crucial role in lifting you to stand authentically on the shoulders of the giants.

It is in knowing your authentic individual that the universe infuses your life with profound freedom, experiences to be grateful for, and people you love and are loved by. Planting, cultivating, and growing seeds that grow your authentic being, reviving your sense of belonging and skyrocketing your growth are what unleashes the freedom in your potential.

The more you start to use the symbiotic relationship of your bipolar nature intelligently, the more you begin to integrate all of your personas into one authentic individual who embraces the authenticity of life itself.

So, before you move on to the next chapter and learn more about principle number two, the questions you may want to answer are these:

Does anyone know the real you – the soul that awaits you patiently behind all the masks? The unfakeable individual that deep down, you know you are? The authentic individual buried behind all the covers you show to the world, which is free from the chains of pain and the illusive façades created by your self-deceptive persona, driven by temptation?

Rewire Your Existential Models of Reality

Principle #2:
Stop Working to Survive, Wake-Up and Thrive

Living to survive and not thrive is an oppressive state. You know this to be true because like me, and like everybody else, you've been there too, fighting to meet your existential needs. You fight to find a shelter you can live in, get an education, a job to pay off your mortgage, and to pay for your food, travel and other essential living costs. Struggling to meet those needs will create a feeling of doubt, loneliness, and low self-worth. So, it's up to you to close the mental gap between your fearful scarcity persona and the abundant, authentic individual that can quickly help you to manifest all that you want to have in your life.

As I am writing this book; all over the world, people are stepping up to meet the COVID-19 pandemic challenges that no human being can escape. Despite having the smartest people in the world working on how to best contain the virus, many people have died. Governments around the world were unprepared for a pandemic of this scale; neither were the long underfunded healthcare systems; and, with the global economy being on the verge of collapse, the livelihoods of millions of people are threatened. There are equally frightening and amazing developments happening every day. One thing is certain; this pandemic will create long-lasting psychological effects, long after the COVID-19 virus has been contained.

If you're stuck at home because of the COVID-19 pandemic, at some point, as your resources deplete, your fears of meeting your existential needs will take over. We saw evidence of this as the shelves of the supermarkets up and down the country were emptied, due to panic buying.

Even the bravest of you out there will experience fears, doubts and have thoughts of how God is punishing you for what you have done or not done. Many of you are thinking that everything that's happening due to the COVID-19s outbreak has a hidden message; a message that says that the Universe wants us to realize something! The earth is taking a break from the pollution, and that we need to take a break from our busy life. You may be right, or perhaps COVID-19 is a message from above and below that we are all at the mercy of our ability to navigate the world's wildest storm, collectively.

Letting your fears run freely through your mind as a result of not meeting existential needs will make you doubt yourself and can paralyse you. Why? Answer: It's because of your make up. It's because the part of your brain that safeguards you from external threats, the amygdala helps you to meet your basic human need, survival.

Not having a job to go to, a clear plan to follow and a vision that inspires you and is carved out for you is what interferes with your instinctual apparatus; the structure that tells you what, where, when, and how you're supposed to act and respond at times of perceived threat.

Have you ever thought about what governs the nature of your existential lived reality?

It is defined by what's in your brain, your experiences, your perceptions and your direct observations. The truth is, many of you go through life with no awareness of the power you possess to rewire your brain, so that it can be in sync with the new reality you want to create. Instead of having a multi-perception awareness of reality, you limit yourself by classifying some of your perceptual experiences as valid, and you dismiss others as illusionary.

Whether or not you realize this, your existential model of reality is strongly influenced by your values, beliefs, perceptions and your view of who you are. If you think you are alone and insignificant, you have more chances of manifesting the reality you want to escape from. If you feel you are part of an expanded reality and grow your awareness of the interconnectedness of all life, you will find yourself in a place where your existential needs are not only met, but are exceeded.

You may be wondering, how would you know what your view of existential reality is?

Consider this scenario: You are having lunch at the airport. You overhear an account of an economy passenger receiving a First Class Upgrade from the next table. What is your initial response likely to be? Would you be cynical? Dubious? Or would you entertain the possibility that this could happen to you too? In other words, is your current existential view 'life is hard', 'I am not lucky', 'first class is only for rich people'. If so then your way of thinking isn't allowing for unusual experiences. Instead of discounting them automatically, you could cancel that thought, change your response, and adopt a new point of view; one that is more empowering such as 'everyday life rewards me with unexpected gifts'. 'I am the captain of my ship and the master of my existential reality'. 'I am thankful for being a money magnet', etc.

Next time you make a judgement, pay attention to the view you may be adopting as your default behaviour. If it's not what you want, silently say *cancel* and change it there and then. The more you learn to do this, the more you will be consciously rewiring your existential models of reality.

If you don't, your present existential models of reality will stop you from growing your life, and being in alignment with the life you want for yourself. You will keep acting, behaving, thinking and feeling in alignment with the very things you want to avoid in your life.

Deep down, you crave the freedom that comes with having your existential needs met, of never having to worry about money, or how to pay bills and purchase those expensive items you always wanted. At the same time, you tend to avoid taking the necessary action needed to build the wealth that can provide you with all those things because of the pain that comes with it.

Avoiding facing the pain that comes with whatever pleasure you are seeking, in this case, an abundance of money, is what keeps you stuck and makes you procrastinate. You observe your reality falsely through rose coloured glasses of the temporarily scarcity masked persona, completely missing the fact that your true authentic self knows that it can create unlimited abundance.

You also know that once your existential needs are fulfilled, you will come to the understanding that the increased personal freedom you just experienced also comes with increased personal responsibility. Suddenly you feel that you are in control of making your own choices and creating your reality. Yet, you are met with a new challenge that you need to overcome that requires you to take on even greater personal responsibility.

The Choices You Make Determines the Reality You Create

Next time you find yourself in front of the mirror, remember, reflections aren't only found in mirrors, but also in everything you observe and perceive. Seeing your actual authentic individual isn't possible unless you take the time to integrate all of your persona's that are safely hidden by the masks you show to the world. It requires a level of awareness that can observe the self in an honest, and non-judgmental way that will helps you to accept your imperfections.

Embrace the duality of your ego and the role it plays in your life, and you'll be able to learn a valuable lesson about your insecurities, judgments and self-deceptive nature. Don't forget: your family traits and how they met their existential needs that you feel are inherited aren't written in stone.

Who you think you are and how you meet those existential needs isn't predetermined? You can re-wire your brain by adopting new beliefs, clarifying your authentic values, and following the five-principles you are learning; to make all the changes you want to make. You just have to start small, and as you become more confident, you will take more significant steps – and then just keep on going.

If you observe most organisms in nature, you will find that they act according to their instincts, making them a part of an inseparable from life. In this state, existential threats and the loneliness arising from the lack of certain things is impossible.

Only if you can see yourself as a separate entity that is in competition against all that is, can you experience fears, loneliness and insecurities arising from dreading not being able to meet your existential needs. The more freedom you have to direct the course of your life, the more this feeling of being separate will gnaw away at you.

In a social order system, if your job is clearly defined for you and you are entirely sure of your place within a society, you feel as if you are a part of something and not apart from something. Your sense of belonging will be secure.

One of the by-products of being an intelligent organism; aware of itself as a separate entity, capable of making its own choices and directing its development, is loneliness. You might be in a better position to be at peace with your loneliness by deciding that this trade-off is worth it.

You will get to experience the world like no other type of organism on the planet does or ever has, you get to decide who you are, but this unique relationship to existence means feeling lonely sometimes.

Existential loneliness is a new concept in existential philosophy, psychology and today's evolution of human consciousness. This sense of perceived emptiness and void arising from what we value reflects a problem within each person, not a lack of meaningful relationships. Many of you may often believe that your profound deficiency is an interpersonal problem.

The existential loneliness that you may feel at times is more deep-rooted than either the absence of a specific person you love or the lack of any meaningful connections with others. Often, many of you may confuse it with problems of love or difficulties of not being in a relationship. You might spend a few years of your life struggling with existential loneliness using methods that are appropriate only for interpersonal isolation.

You might even discover that no matter how good your relationships are, at times, you still feel 'empty' and 'lonesome'. If so, perhaps you are struggling with your existential disease disguised as a complex of problems with money, at work and/or in your relationships.

If you have already tried to solve this problem by improving your relationships, and if you already know that the illusion you hold around what love is may not be the answer to your discontent, perhaps you are ready for rewiring your existential models of reality.

Adopting a new way of thinking is less about your existential loneliness and more about your social isolation that comes from the lack of awareness and grounding of the spiritual energy in this physical experience of life.

The existential loneliness comes from the scarcity persona that hides your real authentic power behind the many façades you've built over a lifetime. And, often, it is a result of the resistance you have created with your basic human need, survival. Maslow's theory on the hierarchy of human needs brilliantly shines a light on your basic survival need for shelter, having a job, making money, feeling safe, and wanting a relationship in which you feel nurtured and grounded.

Every painful experience you may have had in life concerning meeting your existential needs is what created the disempowered scarcity persona you cover up when you are in the presence of people you don't trust and feel unsupported by.

Sharing a justification story is the initial default response of so many of my global clients. They sought my help to rewire their existential models of reality, so as to improve their financial situations and clear their abundance blocks. In repeating the same language, thoughts and story, you have perhaps heard from your parents or other people in your social community, you keep yourself stuck in the energy of lacking something. If you listen carefully to people who lack money but want it, you will keep hearing the same story of why they don't have as much money as they would like to have.

When I consult clients who seek my help to grow their wealth; initially, many of them resist disclosing their current financial state, due to some form of internalised fear. Some clients even feel shameful about talking freely about how much money they don't have, have and or would like to make. Deep down, some also feel that asking how to have more money than the limit they have unconsciously set for themselves is evil. Others find it challenging to make it, receive it, or give it away, without having some form of anger, guilt, or resentment.

Many of you reading this book may cover up the real issue of the lack of money you experience in your life by telling a familiar story, making excuses, or expressing the ingrained belief that 'money does not grow on trees'.

When you wear this façade of lack, you give strength to the poverty persona you may have adopted, that stops you from being unfakably authentic and worth it. Your deceptive-self will make sure that you never expose the real reasons behind why your lack of money is an issue in your life, and face the reality of your financial state. In doing so, you continue to create an existential reality where the fear of lack is more durable than the excitement of creating a new reality in which making a lot of money is comfortable for you.

Working in the corporate world as an information technology executive paid me a six-figure salary, but deep down, I knew I was worth more. Having been made redundant in 2009 from a job I loved, I took some time to examine all of the models of reality I had adopted as real. What I learnt was how limiting my thoughts, language and behaviours around wealth-building were.

The scarcity personas I build throughout my life had created a skewed perception of my true wealth building capabilities. This realisation of my self-deceptive nature trying to align me with my abundant individual self-changed my life forever and for better. It inspired me to re-wire my brain for increasing the money-making limit I had set for myself in my mind, start my entrepreneurial journey, and write what has now become an internationally best-selling and multi-award-winning book: 'A Path to Wisdom'.

In this new reality, that I found myself in 2014, where people from around the world were now paying me my worth to teach them how to go from where they were to where they knew they wanted to be. What I used to make in one year, I was now making in one month, teaching others to make money doing what they love.

Ten years down the line, the COVID-19 global pandemic forced many of us to re-evaluate our lives, to question how we would pay our bills, and make money in the 'post-COVID-19 world'. At times when many are being laid off, just like me; many entrepreneurs and businesses who acted fast made sure that they adapted to the demands of the new environment.

Because of spending ten years building a global business, sharpening my skills, and using the five-principles, I am sharing with you in this book; I was able to turn every challenge presented to me into an opportunity for growth and service, and I adapted fast. I informed all of my global clients that I would henceforth, virtually consult individuals and businesses to help them address the challenges posed by the pandemic, daily. My coaching and consulting business grew despite the fact that 99% of the people around me were sharing doomsday scenarios.

When the World Health Organisation, WHO, announced the global pandemic, and my flights were cancelled. I knew then, that it was time for me to adapt once again; to re-think how to move forward, and re-invent myself. I swiftly created new virtual offerings to my global clients and kept neutralising any negative perceptions as they arose. I very quickly re-wired my brain to function in alignment with the reality I found myself in.

I remember, that on 23 March, after Boris Johnson announced imposing strict restrictions. I reached out to all my clients to establish a need, and then offered them several products and services to help them with their short, medium and long term strategy, to create a road map out of the unprecedented global crisis.

While many people were engulfed by fear and panic, my clients chose to continue to consult with me to assist them to plan, re-invent and offer virtual solutions to a growing crisis quickly. In doing so, their businesses started to source the essential products and services needed to fight the virus crisis and to continue to support their employees.

Your ability to adapt fast and re-wire your brain to find opportunities and blessings in a crisis is what determines how much you can grow and thrive in your personal, professional and business life.

If you are an entrepreneur, a business owner or even someone going through a period of career transition, an external catastrophic event like COVID-19 will evoke a temporary existential crisis in you. Doubt, fear, and uncertainty will then easily creep back into your life. It is then, for instance, that you may have to have a meeting with someone that you want to do business with who can take you to the next step; but you lie and tell them you have no money to pay for such a meeting.

Although in reality, you may have ways to pay for the specific service they offer, deep down, you feel the fear of not having enough, you don't make that critical decision, because some day in your near future you may not have enough money to survive.

When Trust Dies, Mistrust Blossoms

There are many sophisticated protective mechanisms hidden behind your scarcity persona's existential mask, but the one worth considering is the one that was created from your trust in yourself being broken. When there is no trust, there is no faith. Instead, all your doubts start to come out, and your fears begin to weaken your relationship with your authentic, unfakeable being.

Not trusting that part of you that is unfakeable, is interconnected to all life, and can manifest anything you want is what creates incapacitating uncertainty. Everything you think, value, feel and do in life starts to be dictated by the fearful and untruthful scarcity persona hidden behind the 'people cannot be trusted' mask.

When you are feeling uncertain, afraid, and you mistrust your authentic being, you stop believing other people, and you adopt the various scarcity persona behaviours that look to blame and judge others for your misfortunes. You find yourself buried under a cloud of negative thoughts that prevent you from getting the success and the good fortune you deserve.

Not seeing how the ideas of doubt and feelings of limitations can help you grow is what prevents many of you from living your true inspired destiny. A feeling of not having a reliable connection with your unfakeable self-results in no communication ever taking place between you and any person you may be trying to connect, share and collaborate with.

To get my clients to see the importance that trust plays in their lives and in the growth they may be seeking from me, I use metaphors that are familiar to them. Often, I take two mobile phones and I ask someone in the audience to guide us through the process of connecting them so that they can share data between each other.

Depending on how technologically clued-up the person is, they either fail or they succeed. The truth is, if you want to connect two phones to share data, the first step to take is to make sure both devices have their Bluetooth switched on. To pair the device, your phone will start to search for other Bluetooth enabled devices. Once you find the other phone, the authentication process needs to happen before a reliable Bluetooth connection is established. It is during this process that you input the given authentication password, and once the other mobile device has authenticated you, you receive a notification that you are now paired. You currently have a trustworthy connection so that data between two devices can be transmitted and shared.

It is a fact of life that connecting, sharing and collaborating with others is dependent on the invisible authentication and trust process that our physical and emotional bodies can use to connect with one another. There are many clear examples that prove that for things and people to connect, there must be a trustworthy connection. Only when there is a credible connection between you and another individual, can the flow of information happen.

You are the same as a mobile phone. If the trust is broken, no matter how hard you try to communicate with another human being, there will be no connection, collaboration or flow of information. Issues around trust can destabilise your entire personality, your relationships, at work, and with anyone you come into contact with.

Without knowing how to communicate in terms of what builds trust, you will struggle to establish a good connection in which the power of your genuine, authentic individual can grow.

The other aspect that strengthens this elusive and the momentary scarcity persona's façade are times in your life when you have a problematic and unloving relationship with yourself. It is also fortified when your partner and you don't have that trustworthy relationship with each other, your families and others in your social life.

If deep down you feel that there is no trust between you and your parents, no matter what you do, the feeling of abandonment will grow stronger. You will start to feel disconnected from your physical mother, divine feminine energy, and the environment you might find yourself in. You feeling unsafe starts to consume a lot of time in your brain. In each sphere of life, this hazardous feeling will prevent you from creating the trustworthy foundation required for building, living, and thriving with authenticity in the fabric of married life.

The ALARMS to watch out for are: you find yourself having difficulties in being grounded in life, and feeling settled in your work or in any other environment that is different from what you may perceive the norm to be.

Many single men and women who I have helped to attract a fulfilling and trustworthy relationship, often tell me how subconsciously they end up with women or men that remind them of their parents. On many occasions, my female clients say to me how subconsciously, they end up choosing a man that represents unresolved issues they had with their dad or their mother. Often, clients would tell me how they ended up resenting the man they married or dated.

Stop Being a People Pleaser

Through the centuries people have always faced various existential crises; but in today's world, one of the biggest challenges that plague many of us is the idea of your one-sidedness and being perfect. Another challenge is following the latest technology trends and checking your likes on Instagram and other social media every second, to satisfy your attention and people-pleaser scarcity persona seeking external validation.

If you do some research, you will find how years ago, when times were tough, when there was no internet, people had no choice but to be unfakably real with each other. If your child cried all night and the neighbours could hear, they would come and offer help. If you were sick, the whole community knew about it and would offer some kind of support.

If you got married, everyone who knew you, without you sending them any fancy invitation, would come to your wedding to celebrate your special day. And if you were poor, people passing by would give you food, and some people even got lucky and were offered a shelter to spend the night in. This is precisely what happened to me in September 1990 when I was saved from the atrocities of the civil war, and I found myself sleeping rough on the streets of London, with no home to go to or family and friends to turn to for help.

If like me, you were a child in the '70s, or are from an older generation, you would know what I'm talking about. There was no internet, no mobiles, no iPads, no apps, and no email then to use to speak to one another. People used the old fashioned analogue phone to talk to one another, arrange meetings, and agree on times to get together and connect with each other!

These times have been long forgotten, what happened? Nowadays, many of you live your life through social media validation, looking down at your phone's screen, being afraid to greet a fellow passenger on the way to work. The fear of being labelled, judged, mistaken, or ignored is greater than the joy radiating from establishing a heart connection with a fellow human being.

To mask the layers and layers of fabric and brick, credit cards and debts, and frequently attending plastic surgery, many of you use apps to improve the photos you post on various social media and dating sites.

While all of these behaviours that are driven from a temporary scarcity persona looking for validation may have a value, the result is that you're faced with the constant challenge of being real, connecting and sharing your authentic self.

Many of you may feel that you don't even know the difference between what you genuinely care about and what society is forcing you to care about. It's all tangled in a debilitating cycle. In a way, living in a technological cocoon that covers up your pain and shame, you are encouraged to be isolated, lonely, and unloved. Struggling to meet your existential needs leaves you feeling unworthy and unwise enough to skyrocket your achievements. One way to recognise this is to be aware of your behaviours your emotional responses when those feelings arise.

When you disguise your truth, your state of abundance declines and everything else in your life starts to take a downturn. You feel shameful talking about your money issues and you are more likely to judge others who can easily manifest it. You become anxious from thinking that there is not enough money, jobs and clients in the world, and you may feel that sources of abundance are limited.

You continue to live your life from paycheque to paycheque. The energy of the separation from your unfakeable self leads to feeling unworthy of receiving. Another sign of being a people-pleaser to be aware of is not feeling secure in yourself when you have other people around you. Distrust, fear, and rejection are what you start to radiate, and what you attract in your life too.

If you find yourself struggling to meet your existential needs, you also will be afraid. Fear of being judged by others leads to you developing a tendency to withdraw and hide your authentic self behind the masked scarcity persona you adopt at that moment in your life. If no one knows who you are, your masked scarcity persona will stay safe and protected.

If someone's language reveals a lack of confidence, misery and pain, their facial expressions become uninviting to us, though they may be unaware of their body language. At the same time, they may need connections, and their speech may unintentionally communicate "stay away from me."

If in your primary relationship, you are not meeting your existential needs, it can be excruciating for you. You expect to be able to provide safety and support one for another in times of hardship. If you can't, you can lose control, lash out, and turn to self-destructive behaviours that gives you, perhaps, a temporary relief; but, in the long run, ultimately adds more difficulty, pain and struggle for you.

As your capacity to earn money grows, one thing you may want to be aware off is the new scarcity persona that will be emerging. For some of you, a growth in income may increase your desire to separate yourself from those less fortunate who don't make as much money as you do. You start to eat at better restaurants, buy better clothes, drive better cars, live in better homes, belong to specific affluent communities, view yourself as being in a better class, and as part of various groups within which your new-found transient identity can express itself.

Although you may quickly learn how to accumulate material wealth, if you don't learn how to manage the power that money brings, you will lose it. Learning to channel the power increase that wealth brings into your life will help you to continue to grow your authentic power, and ability to live a healthy, wealthy and meaningful life. You mostly spend your daily mental energy in managing the various personas you are learning about in each chapter.

Another good sign to watch for when your people-pleasing persona takes over is the feeling of being unsettled that you are not good enough; and deep down, you don't trust others with their intentions.

What fuels your concern that your existential needs are not being met is not what happens outside of you, but rather all the above issues surfacing inside of you, that include but are not limited to your response to career choices, how you behave at work, and how in touch you are with your unfakeable self when you are trying to find the right work environment that feels nurturing.

Seeing others as potential predators makes you continue to live life through the lens of living your life to meet your basic animal instinct – survival. You focus most of your mental energy in satisfying the need for food, shelter, procreation, money, safety and survival, but not on how to grow your worth and thrive with authenticity.

If companies were able to truly measure the impact that living to survive has on the business world, they would find some shocking figures and facts. What I have noticed in every organisation I have worked and consulted in is the following: When employees come to work as an exchange for a paycheque, engagement, productivity, and inspiration across all departments drops. The overall team morale level is low, and there is distrust that breeds across teams, managers, and senior executive teams. When employees are depressed, feel lonely, and have a head full of noise, they cannot perform at their best, be alert, and become good team players. Often, you will see individuals in the corporate world who work long hours, are feeling burned out, stressed and end up being resentful towards their employers.

The truth is; many unhappy employees, from fear of being laid off, don't speak up about the real source of their company-wide problems. Instead, they avoid disclosing their concerns authentically, creating loneliness and separation that follows them in every part of their daily lives.

Many employees because of the fear of being rejected, ridiculed, or feeling that they are good enough, end up compromising their work-life balance and thus compromise their health.

If you are a leader or an entrepreneur, you know that the real cost to business is much higher than the picture shown by absenteeism and sickness statistics. When a company has disengaged employees who are feeling depressed, it requires additional resources from HR to provide counselling, coaching, support, and ultimately paid sick leave.

The same issues arise from having people go to work disengaged and uninspired can be observed within the health care system, educational institutions, government departments, and in your personal and professional life.

Transform Your Scarcity Persona into a Thriving Individual

Walking your unfakeable path is essential for every one of you. No one but you can construct the bridge upon which you must cross the stream of life precisely; the bridge that connects all your masked personas into one authentic individual – the bridge that is at one with your soul. In making this choice, you let your unfakeable self-enjoy the riches of life.

In having spent thousands of hours developing teams, coaching clients, and consulting businesses and their owners, I have come to observe that people change their scarcity persona behaviours and transform their existential crisis into blessings in unique ways. I encapsulated my findings into the following ten Behavioural Change Principles® (BCP®), so that all of you can use them to change and instil behaviours that make your unfakeable individual thrive in every crucial area in your life.

1. Be adaptable and flexible.
2. Know the role of your fears.
3. Develop emotional intelligence.

4. Differentiate injected from authentic values.
5. Balance one-sided perceptions.
6. Adopt a non-judgmental attitude.
7. Take daily and consistent action.
8. Use repetition, reflection and reinvention.
9. Upgrade your thinking, language, and speaking.
10. Be appreciative, caring, and grateful.

Use the above Behavioural Change Principles® to rewire your brain for the life outcomes you want to create. To increase your chances for the changes you want to happen, take a piece of paper or open a word document and write down what you want to change in your life. You may want to buy a new home, get a new job, build wealth, lose weight, be more in control emotionally etc. Then, list fifty drawbacks and benefits on how each of the principles will help you to achieve your specific outcome.

By the time you write 500 disadvantages and benefits, your brain will be wired to see with equanimity whatever you choose to create, thus inspiring your authentic individual to thrive. The more thorough you are in doing this exercise, the more you'll let the wisdom of your unfakeable self quickly satisfy your growing existential human needs.

The most important thing to realise right now, before you move on to the next chapter, is that your unfakeable individual has the power to make the changes you may be seeking in life, especially living in a world where you barely have a minute to yourself. So, this is a perfect time and way for you to take a moment and complete the following exercise:

- Write down your observation of your met and unmet existential needs. Ask someone who knows you well and see if you can see what's preventing you from breaking free from the pain and the pleasures generated in wearing the 'poor me' mask.

- See if you can recognize in what other forms of not meeting your existential needs shows most in your daily life. Notice in which specific area in your life your scarcity persona shows up most, with whom, why, and what purpose it serves you. For instance, it may bring to your awareness that you may have the material wealth you are seeking in a different form, i.e. unused intellectual property.
- List the experiences you are limiting yourself to in all of the eight critical areas of life, by letting your survival instinct take over, that is not being able to pay for that five-star hotel where you want to stay, the course you want to do, or the coach-mentor you wish to have in your life.
- Identify in which life experiences you feel most segregated, isolated, lonely, and rejected. Is it with people who have more of what you want? Or perhaps, in your intimate relationships, at work, or with your family?
- Is your default response to continually complain about money and the lack of same? Or is it about relationships, being fearful about your future, or not trusting people? Could it be that you repeatedly tell people about your life struggles and not being able to find the right job?

Once you have completed this exercise, close your eyes, take a few deep breaths and start to reflect on each one of them. Open your eyes, make sure that you write down all of the lessons you can draw from completing this exercise with their appropriate follow-up actions.

Disarm Your Emotions

Principle #3:
Disarm Your Emotional Field to Build an Impenetrable Shield

Using your emotions intelligently is a choice you are capable of making. You can either let them weaken or strengthen the power of your unfakeable self. It is up to you what choice you make, but to unleash the authentic power, you need to build the skills and the strength required to disarm your emotions. It is wise to use your feelings as a sophisticated alarm and guiding system that your inner unfakeable warrior can use to protect and safeguard you when you need it the most.

Your inner soldier's fighting capabilities can either be lessened or increased by how you perceive your reality and the many heart-breaking, heart-wrenching events that happen to you over a lifetime. The pain accumulated by any skewed perceptions you may hold on too is what puts you into a never-ending emotional roller coaster, and that is what weakens the real power of your unfakeable self.

Why? Because, with passing time, the memories with their associated one-sided perceptions of specific painful life experiences are solidified into your emotional body and into your mind. You start to find it challenging to know, deal and neutralise your undesired feelings related to some event in the past or an event that may happen in the future. You feel as if you have lost control of your built-in emotional guiding system, resulting in profound and persistent feelings of abandonment, resentment and unworthiness.

Sometimes, you may even have difficulties because your view of yourself is inferior or undeserving. Being ashamed about who you think you are in a specific moment in your life blocks you from connecting meaningfully with yourself and others.

If you feel you are becoming dysregulated emotionally by an outside stimulus, it is because you think that at that moment you have lost control of your feelings. Feeling insecure about your life can also lead to experiencing a lack of emotional stability and security. Perceiving danger everywhere around you makes you less likely to be open in acknowledging someone else's perspective and views on life.

Introversion, self-consciousness, shyness and difficulty with approaching people to initiate conversations and to build a long-lasting, trusting relationship are just some of the clear signs of an out of control emotive persona to watch out for.

When your emotive persona takes over, you start to avoid communicating with others at all costs, because you think that interacting with them may result in conflicts; and conflicts in a relationship may lead you to falsely believe that the relationship has 'failed' in some way.

Frequent feelings of being mistaken and misunderstood can leave you with a sense of low self-esteem, self-worth, and self-conscious about your pitfalls. A deceptive belief that you are rejected. This is a hard mask to take off, as you may not be able to identify the mechanisms your one-sided emotive persona is using to hide your unstoppable and unfakeable true self. A sign to look for is the tendency to blame both yourself and others about your life troubles, lack of success and unhappiness.

Usually, when you put on this emotive persona mask, to others, you appear as defensive and ineffective at managing and self-regulating your emotions, and you will find it hard to build authentic- relationships. You say things like "you hurt me". "You are making me angry". "It's your fault for ..." etc. For everything you are unhappy in your life you point the finger at other people, and at external circumstances you have no control over; disregarding that in doing so, you give your power away to others. Forgetting one crucial life rule, when you point your index finger to blame someone outwardly, you thumb points to God, and the little, ring, and middle fingers are pointing back at you.

Your emotive persona may make you feel reluctant even to try and take new responsibilities at work, take part in group activities, and say 'no' to people and things, leaving you feeling exploited and weak. Most of the time, hidden from your awareness, this emotive persona can make you self-centred, appear egotistical, and force you to think only about yourself and no one else.

You may feel that you are doing this to protect your true feelings, but if you don't do something about it, the negative karma you keep creating, but with time, it increases the pain you feel.

For those of you who may not know the meaning of the word Karma, it comes from the Sanskrit word kri: कृ. It means 'to do' or 'to act'. Although many compare it to Newton's law of cause and effect, simply put it, whatever you put into the universe will come back to you. So, it is prudent to choose what you put out with your thoughts, language, and actions.

Through years of working with clients to disarm themselves and strengthen the emotional shield of their unfakeable self, I have observed a pattern of overlooking or failing to see how the deep-rooted emotional pain that they never addressed adequately and actually weakens them.

If like me, for whatever reason, you were forced to leave home at a very young age, the warrior of your transient emotive persona, would have either weakened or strengthened. This would have depended on how skewed the emotional imbalances created from feeling uncertain, and disconnected from the environment in which you once felt safe, were.

Feeling homesick, nostalgic, or perhaps abandoned, uncared, and unloved is just a side effect of undergoing a drastic change. In my instance, from experiencing being forcefully removed from a safe family environment and put into a brand new context, my inner emotive warrior knew nothing about it.

The danger here is this, behavioural negativities due to an emotional crisis may increase without you ever looking at the root cause of such change. Subconsciously, you create the emotive persona that quickly puts on a mask when similar experiences show up in your future.

Stop Being a Slave to Your One-sided Emotions

Many of you may be challenged by your emotive persona, by the loneliness it creates in your life and by impeding your overall achievements in life. No matter your age or your intelligence, being submissive to your emotions wastes opportunities for connection, collaboration and friendship. And for many of you, it may cause unbearable deep pain.

Letting your feelings weaken your unfakeable self is something that we all suffer from in varying degrees. Thus, understanding the fundamental characteristics of your emotive persona enables you to identify it in yourself, as well as recognizing it in others.

An excessive emotional outburst is a human response that develops out of apprehension. Once it is identified what triggers are the cause, new empowering behaviours can be instilled in you, and its effects can be reduced and in some cases fully diminished.

Decreasing the intensity of your emotional reactions puts you on a path to mastering your emotional guidance system. It is what improves the quality of your life, your overall wellbeing, your wealth and your relationship with yourself and the people around you.

Sentiments can hide the truth from your awareness. Everything that creates them in the first instance and whatever is associated with that hidden feeling of discomfort can make you feel that you are all alone in the world, and act like you are in a vast vacant place, all alone, even if in reality, you are in a roomful of people.

Things to look out for when your emotive persona silently takes over your unfakeable authentic self is a pain in your chest, heaviness in your heart, and a deep sinking feeling in your stomach. The sentiment is sitting on top of the belief or firm conviction, especially in moments of severe emotional pain and longing that no one understands, no one gets it, and no one ever could. Even though it is not necessarily true, sometimes, it melts into self-pity, anger, sadness, grief, depression and hopelessness.

What follows is often a feeling of giving up, or it awakens the emotive rebellion and warrior in you. If in those moments you think, 'forget it, why even bother?' or 'that's it, I give up, I'm out of here', you give in to the power of your transient emotively driven persona.

You start to entertain the idea that you are worthless and undeserving of love; or that, the person who has hurt you is unworthy of your love, and then you blame them for being incapable or unwilling to give you what you need. Either way, you feel the pain and the hurt, and you end up giving your authentic power away.

Sometimes the pain arising from not being in control emotionally may last for a few seconds or a few minutes, but they may even last a few hours, or in the worst case scenario they may become chronic and last for a long time.

For many of you, this pain comes and goes, and it's not unusual to feel emotional, even in the best of times in your life. Though you may wish it, the truth is, you cannot be in control of your emotions all the time; because of the duality of your nature. If you expect things to be one-sided, pain without pleasure, you are setting yourself to even more hurt. This addiction to embracing only what we perceive as true is what often eclipses all of the meaningful and fulfilling things that may exist in critical areas of your life.

There are options, of course.

See Emotional Crisis as a Blessing in Disguise

You do not have to suffer, although sometimes it may seem as if it is your mantra that you are meant to hurt. You can decide to take good care of yourself, not just when you respond objectively, but also when you are emotional about events and when self-negative talk takes over.

History has taught us over and over that there is no crisis without a blessing. When confronted with the need to meet the challenges presented by a crisis with clarity, creativity, open-mindedness, and open-heartedness, you are required to upgrade your mind's ability to cultivate those qualities to more fully exemplify them in making the decisions and taking the actions that will serve your well-being and that of others best. The key to doing this lies in the actual definition of the word 'crisis'. It comes from the Greek, 'Krisis', which means; 'a turning point in an illness that can mean either recovery or death'.

What's interesting is that in the Chinese language, the term for crisis is represented with two characters, which translates into 'danger' and 'opportunity'.

Because you usually associate a crisis with danger, many of you often forget that each crisis contains the seeds of opportunities for growth, learning, healing and previously unrecognized possibilities. If you choose, every crisis you may experience offers gifts that can enlighten and inspire you to look outside of the box that contains your tried and genuine responses to stressful and threatening situations.

Using this fact of life to see how whatever is happening to you emotionally also comes with hidden benefits. Talking things out with someone you trust and know can be of great support to you. It is advisable to write it all down in a journal, go for a long walk, or observe the benefits of the crisis quietly in meditation by breathing deeply, rhythmically and being present to all that is.

You can acknowledge to yourself that whatever situation you perceive as emotionally hurting you is also benefiting you, and most likely, unaware to your conscious self it has some form of hidden pleasure attached to it. In adopting an objective view, you can study it, learn what, when and how it happened, who observed it at that moment and see how it served you.

Practising this acknowledgement process regularly makes you a great detective of your skewed perceptions that fire up your irrepressible emotive persona. The better you become at seeing the blessings in times of emotional crisis, the more unfakeable you become. The more emotions you neutralise, the better you feel about yourself, and the more of your authentic power you unleash. As you learn to work with your emotions intelligently, you consciously take actions, do things, and direct your energies toward what makes you succeed in life.

Your uncontrollable emotive persona can equally negatively impact your intimate relationships and your marriage. Many of the individuals and couples who I have worked with, fundamentally, all showed signs of having an unrealistic expectation of who the other person in the relationship must be, needed to be or should be.

Yes, it takes work to untangle the protective mechanisms of your emotional persona, but if you remain committed and consistent, you too can be in a fulfilling and growing relationship. Whatever emotional blockages you may have, you can neutralise them by identifying and disarming your emotions.

Yes, it can be done, just the way I have done it usually using the same principles I am sharing here, you too can do it. It is why I felt called to write The Unfakeable Code®, and be there ready for you. Available, when you are called and willing to do the inner work required for you to integrate all of the disempowered personas, you are learning more about in each chapter into one authentic individual; the one who is unfakeable, the one whose authentic power can help you get closer to the things you want in your life, and most importantly, the person who is there for you the most – the unfakeable you.

It is up to you to choose to disarm your emotive persona; but, in making that choice, you take back control of the direction your life is going in. You will learn to go easier on yourself and others, and you will find that you get much more of what you need and want.

Holding on to a truth derived from biased opinions and unbalanced perceptions is what stops millions of you from loving what you have falsely made yourself to believe as unlovable.

Attending Dr. John Demartini's Breakthrough Experience was a great confirmation of years of research and coaching thousands of my global clients using The Unfakeable Code® and the TJSeMethod: ALARM® conscious mind engineering principles to acknowledge the presence of love in everything they have not loved. In doing so, they achieved a breakthrough with lifelong results and brought about miracles in their life.

Seeing John creating the same effect on people made me realise that I was on the right track. I no longer was alone in teaching and concluding that it is impossible to see the interconnectedness of all life, the blessings in crisis, and experiencing an original state of love if the lens through which we perceive our reality is one of judgment. That is something that the Sufi, Bektashi leaders my parents used to take me to also used to teach me as I was growing up.

Disempowered states of awareness are the places where all of your one-sided perceptions love to hide, thrive and further thicken the self-made poignant prison walls that safeguard the truth from you. In such states, you falsely believe that you are very far away from being the loving, and encompassing unfakeable human being that you were born to be and know you can be.

Addiction to the one-sided emotional persona can bring your entire immune system down, create chemical imbalances and reactions in your body and ultimately, it can make you ill. Living with an addiction to the single expectation of self makes you very good at hiding your feelings, and when challenged, you become very angry at showing them.

When your physical immune system is compromised due to a one-sided illusion of self, routine healing does not take place if your perceptions about what pains you are out of balance. Often, when I am with a client, speaking at an event or interviewed on TV or a radio show about how to improve our spiritual, mental, emotional, physical health, relationship, social, business and financial wellbeing, I share the following:

Any improvement you want in your life is the result of upgrading your psychology in alignment with the outcomes you want in your life.

You cannot heal, improve or transform your life experience with the same psychology that created the problems you want to avoid in the first instance. When your sense of security or integrity of authentic character is compromised, it becomes hard for you to be emotionally together, and most likely, you will struggle to be true to yourself. Instead, like a hungry lion, your emotive and uncontrollable vulnerable persona goes into attack mode each time, and the values you uphold high are challenged.

The more polarised you become, the less likely it becomes for your healthy immune system to discern between what is toxic and harmful and nurturing and loving. The healthy emotional immune system knows of your unfakeable self, and it knows when you are not being true to yourself. If you put on a mask, you'll perceive things only as challenging, harmful or benign.

Continuing to ignore what your emotional wellbeing is asking of you, leads to your bodily functions being compromised. To the outer world just like my client John's story you read earlier on, you may be perceived as if 'you have it together', but inside there is that feeling that knows of your ignorance of what prevents you from seeing within you what is out of balance.

When the pain is too big to handle, your emotional guidance system spirals out of control. It starts to act in a similar way as a mobile phone would when trying to find a location without a satellite GPRS signal being available.

No matter which direction you point your mobile phone in, it will keep telling you that the phone is unable to connect and ultimately stop you from reaching your desired destination. In the same way, due to your emotive masked persona being armed and ready to attack, your unfakeable self would not be able to find the desired direction and purposefully move forward. In adopting the fact that there is a blessing for every crisis attitude, you too can see your direction, happiness and meaning in life.

In neutralising your perceptions, you disarm your feelings, which in turn, allows you to find and discover within yourself all of the disowned parts that you judge in others and have rejected within yourself.

One-sided perceptions that give rise to your emotive persona can cause you to create a new transient identity that separates your unfakeable self from the rest of your friends, family and the community you were born into. They can swiftly hide your authentic self behind a cultural, social, or extreme religious masked persona that you briefly adopt.

What Does Your Relationship with Food Say About You?

You may be aware that there is growing scientific evidence that shows how your relationship with yourself impacts your relationship with food. You may even believe that the only sure way of being is what you have been told so far – that you are only allowed to eat certain foods, which causes your immune system to weaken in the long run. You may falsely believe that you have a closer bond with particular types of people who have similar emotive personas as you, and you may end up in an intimate personal relationship with them.

Your relationship with a similar emotive persona may also give birth to another separation from your true authentic self. The feeling is so strong that you change your habits to please them, and you start to label yourself using the same terms as they do such as Agonistic, Vegan Warrior, Vegetarian, Carnivore, Fish Eater, Kosha, Halaal, etc. And, before you know it, you forget who you were before you knew what those labels meant.

For some of you that may adopt those transient identities, having a strict diet based on the fears of your emotive persona, and not from having accepted certain medical facts and listening to your body's intelligence; which may not be the best thing for you, as you may have been led to believe. Your body intelligently knows what to eat, when to eat, and how much to eat at any given moment. Thus, listening to the ALARM's of your body is essential to your physical health as such alarms are the feedback mechanisms that your body is using to bring about the healing power of your unfakeable self.

Be aware of food restrictions that some of you may create as a result of taking on other people's values, morals, ethics and beliefs. You need to remind yourself of the importance to remain objective when you make individual lifestyle choices. The same people whose values you may be adopting, may have developed certain conditions due to hardships they may have come up against in their own lives. If that is the case, as your awareness increases, you may realize that the values you adopted from them may have nothing to do with your circumstances.

Having an unhealthy relationship with your body also deregulates your healthy digestive system, the one that intuitively it knows what type of food it requires to function at optimum levels. There is plenty of scientific research available that you can read to help you to further your knowledge of the link between emotions, particular types of foods and certain behaviours.

Some clients I have helped to reduce their body weight saw obesity as their body's way of emotionally protecting them from hurt and harm. In gaining weight, they felt unattractive and thereafter, unconsciously they put on weight as a protective mechanism to keep people away from them. Other clients I have worked with, would share how they gained weight from the fear of being abandoned, hurt, and rejected again. Others, said they had gained weight due to hormonal imbalances, lifestyle choices, and stress.

The more polarized your opinions, language and the thoughts you think are, the more you create multiple layers of inner separation, which then prevents you from being in control of your emotions. Some clients have used what I am sharing throughout the book to heal allergies and food intolerances. Any physical symptom you may have is a specific message from your body to you to bring into your awareness what you need to change in your life.

The more biased you are, the less you can see the true nature of your unfakeable and infinite being, and the further away you become from being the master of your emotional guidance system, and ultimately the freedom you are seeking. It is this emotional concealment that makes you separate yourself from others. It is also what makes some of you feel the pressure of having to procreate, become a parent, and fulfil societal, family and religious expectations of you.

If you pay attention to your emotions in any given moment, you can find how it is you who plants emotional weeds in the garden of your mind. It is you who further stimulates the discord you feel within between the parent, the adult and the inner child in you. For those of you who are interested in how these internal transactional analyses can positively or negatively impact your life, you may want to grab a copy of 'A Path to Wisdom' and read it over and over again until you master how to use the method to go deeper within yourself and learn to manage your emotions and mental states better.

One of the parent clients I worked with was very critical of his children. As time went by, the children developed addictive personalities, learned to be people pleasers, and were labelled introverted and shy. When I observed their children outside their home environment, they showed themselves to be extroverted, dangerous, reckless and disobedient; a pattern that follows many children into their adult lives. While I was teaching the parents how to use the Behavioural Chane Principles® I mentioned in the previous chapter, a method I use to instil new parenting behaviours; they started to transform their language, to avoid criticism and instead they used objectivity as a way to appreciate, communicate, and transform their relationship with their children.

Many of you may have parents who are either in love with one another, are divorced or, fight like cats and dogs, most of the time. Some parents may have such full schedules that they come home tired and flop down on the couch to watch television. With no energy left to listen to their children's dilemmas, they never take the time to understand their wants or their needs. And when parents don't listen to their children's problems, the children learn to hide away behind a disempowered emotive persona that tells them 'you don't matter'. No matter how much the children may try to explain, they start to feel that their parents can't help them to overcome the hysterical emotive persona wanting attention, love, or just someone to hear them (you probably already knew that was the case before I even said it!).

Master Your Emotions and Save a Life

You go through a moment in your life when you are afraid to tell your friends and the people that you are concerned about your inner turmoil, discords, and fears. You're scared to tell them the things that are bothering you inside, because deep down you're afraid that they will think you are needy or weird, and that you may end up losing them. So, the voice of your elusive emotive persona tells you that you can't trust your friends, nor can you believe those inner messages that come from your fears of being left all alone. You are not alone in feeling this way. Many young people often feel as lonely as a bird sitting on top of a house! No wonder J.D. Salinger, an American writer best known for his novel 'The Catcher in the Rye', after the public attention and scrutiny he got, became a recluse, withdrawn and weird! With our lives being on display for the public to scrutinise on every social media platform invented, it is no wonder so many young people attempt or end up committing suicide!

Statistics published indicate that suicide among young people and teenagers is skyrocketing. Why? It's because we simply can't live isolated in a virtual world without real friendship, real touch and genuine love. We can't live in a world of endless fake-ness, hiding behind the masked personas that cover our true unfakeable self who yearns for meaningful belonging, connection, and love. That's why so many young people spend most of their time on social media, go and wander around in a shopping mall, join groups, gangs, tribes, live on the streets, or retreat into clubs. They have nothing else to do – but 'hang out'. There are lights there. People are moving around. It helps a little towards numbing the pain, but not much! If you are not careful, the masks of your emotive persona can leave you feeling alone in a crowd and in the world!

Before you move onto the next chapter, I invite you to take a moment and do this transformational exercise. Write your answers in as much detail as you can, reflect on them and on what you have learnt so far.

- Write about an experience where your emotive warrior made you fight, fly or freeze.
- Make a note about which experience you feel mostly contributed towards charging your feelings of being emotionally isolated, lonely, and rejected.

- Describe the person who triggered the most rage or joy in you.
- What observations can you make about the person who challenges your emotions the most?
- Recognize in what forms the same observations show up in other areas in your life.
- Now ask yourself the question; what do rage and joy tell you about yourself?
- Write down; why you responded the way you did?
- What emotional biases can you observe in your answers? Do the same preferences come up in other experiences in your life? or, do your emotive personas keep inventing new ones?
- Make a list of all of your conscious and unconscious emotive intentions.
- Write down the shortcomings your transient emotive persona brings into your life.
- Through reflective awareness, write down what the emotive persona says about you and your emotional wellbeing.
- Write down all the blessings, and benefits your emotive disempowered and empowered warrior brings into your life.
- And finally, what would you gain in your life by disarming your emotive persona letting your authentic being connect, engage and share with others lovingly?

By answering the questions above in as much detail as you can think of, you can neutralise your emotive persona with the knowledge required to arm your unfakeable, and authentic, emotive warrior with an impenetrable love shield that protects you from the one-sided illusion that your emotive persona wants you to live by. Use the process above as many times as you want, to turn the same emotive warrior into a mindful ambassador who uses and manages emotions intelligently to help you take back control, unleashes your worth, and lets you live authentically and freely on your own terms.

Stop Giving Your Power Away, Own it

Principle #4:
Taking Back Control is an Inside Job

It's a fact of life; no one around you can gift you power. The transient power that comes from being awarded a degree from a prestigious university, being promoted at work, being elected as an executive in a Fortune 500 company, and perhaps even worshipped as the leader of a country or a religion you may belong to, eventually dissipates over time.

You may be given as many influential roles as you can think of. Millions of people may assume that you have power, but your unfakeable, authentic self knows the truth. It knows that you don't own the power given to you, for it can disappear out of your life as quickly as it came.

Any external power received from an outside authority is transient. History is a great teacher. All we have to do is to acknowledge this illusion. Look at what happened to the presidents, leaders and legendary people who have come and gone. Celebrated scientists are no different. Likewise, once celebrated philosophers, famous musicians, actors, and anyone else you observe as powerful because of titles they may have been given also come and go.

Real authentic power does not come from an external source, but from harmonising the duality of your nature, giving rise to the power of the unfakeable individual within you. You are born with incredible power, yet, at some time, perhaps in your childhood, you started to give it away. With time, due to the emotional pain, shame and disappointments that life throws at you, you lost sight of who you are and the courage you once had.

Usually, through no fault of your own, you failed to develop an authentic, durable, and robust sense of self. Instead, what you learnt is how to use the many coping and protective mechanisms hidden behind an impulsive persona's façade you show to the world to project a false sense of self.

One day, you will wake up from the illusion you have been living in and you will realize that the price of giving your authentic power away is too high to pay and that it is no longer worth it. The voice within, your body's ALARM's will not stop clamouring at you until you make YOU the most critical person in your life.

Like me, many of the thousands of people who I have helped, and many of you, at some point in your life, will realize that in giving your power away you are betraying your authentic self. You are dishonouring your authentic values, wants and needs.

Surely you can remember the pain you may have experienced during those dating years, or perhaps when you were in a relationship that you couldn't wait to get out of – being with family members that yell at you or even being surrounded by colleagues, friends or groups of people who you feel infuse you with their negative energy; and, who make it their mission to control what you say or do.

Mirror, Mirror on the Wall, Whose More Controlling of Them All?

The actual colours of other people's transient masked personas are revealed when you turn the pressure meter on. When they no longer get what they want from you, they start to display controlling, narcissistic, and egocentric behaviours.

Unless you are a trained professional who is being paid to help these people create breakthroughs – to create the freedom that you want in your life, stay away from the people who try to tear down people who build others up.

What some of you may forget is how the destructive, mean or otherwise heartless behaviour you observe in others you also exhibit to them in other forms or with other people. Other people's responses are there because something is going on with them that you judge is in you.

Many of my clients say:, "It's your/their fault."

"They must stop doing this."

"Oh, my husband and children make me SO mad."

"My colleague is so annoying."

"You are mean," etc. – but the reality is that people who exhibit these harmful behaviours are showing an outward display of inward pain. While some of you may feel that pain gets inflicted in your life, the truth is, the pain that's in you is because of your interpretation of it. It is that part of your wounded, and impulsive persona that is calling for you to heal and love it and others.

Yes, it's hard when someone is shouting at you, not listening to you, forgets your anniversary, or your birthday, or you feel that they are trying to undermine you and what you stand for; being pointlessly vicious, ignoring what's important to you, etc. What's worth remembering is this; it is the voice of their pain, speaking to your pain.

Unfortunately, when you don't know this critical fact when you are pointing the finger of blame outwardly, you are giving your authentic power away. You let their pain strengthen the pain you have forgotten to heal within yourself. In doing so, their discomfort becomes your agony. You ruminate for hours, days, months, and some of you may do so for years.

You must make it your mission to find ways to deal with the people who you perceive have power over you the next time you encounter them. Some of the clients who I have helped to transform their impulsive persona into a powerful individual, tell me how they fantasize about saying just the best thing to knock them off their game. At some of the events where I have spoken, I heard people say that they went to the extent of acquiring a voodoo doll and sticking pins in it each time they felt threatened by someone.

One of the signs to look for if you are truly giving your power away is what is going on in your mind and with your emotions. How much of your day do you spend thinking negative thoughts, and using language that blames others for your misfortunes in life? Pay attention to where you focus your energy most of the time when you are interacting with someone who you perceive is displaying negative behaviour.

Do you keep your mind focused on what they have said (or not said) to you, what they have heard (or not heard), what they have done (or not done), or do you take control of your perceptions of it, and choose the meaning it has to offer their lives or your life?

The problem in trying to change others in the direction of feeling powerful is that you have no power over what the other person says, does, hears or perceives. You can't change that; only they can change that. No matter how much you ruminate on the subject, whatever you judge in them it is not going to change, unless they take charge of it themselves.

No matter how hard you try to say 'just the right thing', it won't shift their unhealed pain, their unhappiness, and their dissatisfaction with themselves, unless maybe like me, you are a qualified and trained professional who can help.

You can only stop the cycle of giving your power away by meeting your unfakeable self, the self that has mastered the dark and the light of your impulsive persona and has integrated them into one authentic individual. As you learn to use all of the principles of the unfakeable code on your daily life, you will see clearly, that the virus of the modern age that I talk about in '#Loneliness'; is your addiction to getting rid of the half of your persona that you judge and tell not to love.

Here is a challenge. Next time you encounter someone who's terrible behaviour is challenging you, makes you feel harmful and controlled, consider finding out what masked persona's and their associated traits you judge in them and have not loved in you. This simple yet powerful exercise can help you take back control, and most importantly, not give away your power.

Adopt Pain and Pleasure in Equal Measure Attitude

Realize that you can own your perceptions, reactions and the meaning you attach to what is shown in your outer reality. In recognizing this, you have the power to shift the energetic exchange and diminish the hurt inflicted by what you label as 'energy vampire', 'negative person', 'battery drainer', and so on.

It is true, in one way or another, we have all been there, in a place where our powerless masked persona gave our power away, where we have often asked ourselves is it worth it. Yet, it takes years to build the inner awareness, resilience and the strength required to own your power. But, in time you'll realize it's worth any energy, money and time you spend on helping you build it.

The truth is, all of the life-changing events, people, and situations that I once felt took every inch of my power were in actuality the most significant catalyst for my transformation like it often is in life.

Many of us want to avoid the pain at all costs and embrace the pleasures life brings quickly. But, it is a pain that sharpens our character, makes us find the once-forgotten inner strength, and forces us to make difficult decisions that often lead to radical changes in your life.

While you may initially see how self-absorbed, self-obsessed, self-admiring, self-involved, and selfish people who take away your power are, with acknowledging the part you play in it, you awaken a new awareness. One that knows you are what you observe in others, it's up to you to do the work to own the traits that you judge or admire.

No matter how long you choose to live with the illusion that others are to blame for all the pitfalls, you may experience in your life, at some point, life itself will force you to see the real picture. The one that is aware of the role your impulsive persona plays in your journey to becoming unfakeable. It is those wounded parts of our various personas hidden behind the countless masks we are afraid to show to the world from the fear of not being loved for all that we are and are not. Not the illusion that is created by struggling to maintain the impulsive persona's false façade, but the truth that your authentic self and your soul hidden behind all the masks knows.

By avoiding accepting your bipolar nature you give more power to your unhealthy, and one-sided ego-self. It's what I call 'the egotism of your wounded personas'.

To compensate, you develop what's called a 'false sense of self'. The severity and the intensity of your impulsive false-self persona depends on the degree of how polarized your thinking is. In desperate pursuit of a sense of self, you get used to telling lies about yourself. You may either exaggerate or minimise things about who you are, what you do, and what you are capable of doing.

Be aware. If you repeat untrue things about yourself often enough, they become the 'truth' that you may know about you until a trained professional helps you to break this illusion about yourself. This was also the case with my client Paul McMonagle, who, at the beginning of his coaching and healing journey showed extremely polarized opinions about himself, healthcare professionals, his family, friends, and the people who he worked with. Living for twenty or so years with epilepsy, OCD and other mental health issues made him turn to various addictions, even to the point of attempting to commit suicide on multiple occasions in an effort to rid himself of the excruciating pain he felt deep down.

Your authentic self is the core of who you are, and it is the unfakeable individual who consistently integrates the countless dark night's and light angel's power-hungry personas into one. It is this individual who knows your soul. It is not the one-sided persona that people tell you should, must and need to be nor is the 'you' defined by people who do not even know you: the doubters, judges, critics, and others who see the part of you that in themselves they have not loved.

The disowned part of yourself that you have not owned is your one-sided ego warrior persona's tool that it uses to control others. They make you appear as strong or weak when you talk about you to the people who know you best and whom you trust to be careful with your vulnerabilities.

The unfakeable individual, the one who is living authentically, always thrives on creating quadruple triple win-win-win-win solutions and outcomes. Win for others, society, themselves and humanity. The more you stand in your power, naturally, your approach to conflict resolution is to think, do and act in ways that serve all parties, you, the other person, the people around you, and the broader circle in which you live and work. You also understand how by being your authentic self, you make it possible for others to do the same.

In learning to stand authentically with one another we can amplify the healing power of love, and find solutions to humanity's current and future challenges.

After all, when you are living as the unfakeable self, your intuition is the strongest, and you can receive inner guidance that directs you to take actions in alignment with your authentic values and benefits humankind and all sentient beings. This means not only that you don't sacrifice your own needs for another, but you also don't disregard those of others for the sole benefit of serving you.

The thinner the layer of your impulsive persona's false self-façade is, the more reliable the power of your authentic individual becomes. Your self-reflective awareness makes you examine how your expectation of others leads to disempowering behaviours, and its impact on others. You strive to take high priority actions that are in alignment with your authentic values and for the benefit of others and the world in general.

With thriving to be unfakeable, you start to listen to the voice of your trustworthy individual – the one who realizes the existence of the unbreakable connection with all that is. And, in harming another or some aspect of the universe, you are actually hurting yourself.

In letting your impulsive persona control the way you observe your reality, you end up creating a false sense of self that believes that you can't afford to be vulnerable at all, especially not to yourself. Be aware of the illusion created by the lies of your impulsive persona's one-sided ego. So, you make up a fictitious, false self-persona who is everything the narcissist is not: the entitled, superior, inflated, and grandiose self-fed by the narcissist's fantasies and what they can squeeze out of sources of narcissistic supply.

This mask, which some of you may think is real, hides the damaged, hurt and insecure part of yourself and chases away feelings of abandonment, depression, rejection and shame. It temporarily protects you from painful emotions – it reinforces affirmations of the false self to keep the impulsive persona's mask in good repair and as we, the British people would say, 'keep calm and carry on'.

If you're not forthcoming, you demand them in one way or another in the ways that make any relationship you have with yourself or others a wild ride on a never-ending emotional rollercoaster.

When I read the 'Malignant Self-Love: Narcissism Revisited', the author Sam Vaknin's words, "The false self serves as a decoy, it attracts the fire." It made perfect sense.

I understood how all of the masked personas and their associated self-deceptive mechanisms act as a proxy for the true self. Our one-sided ego can become as tough as concrete or a nail that can absorb any amount of pressure, weight, and punching.

By giving in to those false personas, your inner child, adult and parent develop immunity to the indifference, manipulation, sadism, smothering, or exploitation. In short: to the abuse, inflicted on you by other people and primary objects in life.

The next time you find yourself feeling that you are being attacked, the impulsive persona that you choose to show to the world at that moment acts as a cloak, protecting you, rendering you invisible and omnipotent at the same time.

As you learn to uncover the truth behind this impulsive persona's façade that makes you feel helpless, first of all, you come to acknowledge that you are the creator of this false self-persona. Therefore, you deserve better, painless, more considerate treatment. The false self, thus, is a mechanism intended to alter other people's behaviour and attitude towards the narcissist.

The problem with the false self-façade is that it takes a lot of energy and work to keep the fragile, superficial mask in good enough shape to protect you daily against potential 'attacks' coming from the outside world. You give in to your self-absorbed ways of handling those attacks, especially those from formerly excellent sources of supply like people you hang out with, work with or date as well as spouses and children.

Choosing to destroy this illusion will force many of you to take a closer look at yourselves, which let's face it, is terrifying. That's why you protect the one-sided impulsive persona's ego mask so aggressively in ways that makes you continually doubt yourself. It's harrowing to have your feelings rejected by someone whom you feel or have felt so much love for, but, it is also remarkably freeing.

Don't Be Convinced By Your Arguments, But By Your Sincerity

While your life may be dominated by doing, achievement, and performance, it is equally important to nurture honest relationships with others. This is one reason why you see so many single people at high levels in organizations or in careers in which they get a lot of attention, such as politics, entertainment, and the ministry.

The job perk of being essential and lauded is irresistible to the false-self, the unhealthy part of your impulsive, arrogant persona, denying you the joy you may find in a fulfilling relationships that may be at home longing for you.

While this truth may make you furious, keep in mind how the layers of defence and self-deception are so intense that, when your impulsive persona wears this disempowered ego façade, you can no longer tell the difference between lies and the truth.

The narcissist part in you genuinely believes its formerly reliable sources. In this way you have succumbed to the old 'bait and switch' and adopted another mutilated impulsive persona. This was the case with my client Paul, who not only did not see the trap he was in, but felt helpless in ripping the false-ego mask from his face without hurting himself and the people he cared about in the process.

It took many sessions for Paul to consider the possibility that the Ying Yang balance concept he knew existed on the outside also lived on the inside. To not be convinced by his arguments, but by the integrity existing deep down, he knew he had that balance. During this process, he learned to be aware of the role the biased opinions that made him angry and resentful played, in satisfying the many layers of his self-protecting mechanisms.

The more he used each principle of The Unfakeable Code™ you've been learning about, the more he rewired his models of reality and adopted a more objective view about people, situations and life in general. He saw how many of his friends and family members were still holding on to the cover of the hurt impulsive persona they had built over many years of suffering from various mental health issues. Not only did they did not see how investing in his personal development was helping him change his ways; some of them made it their mission to attack him back as he started unpeeling the layers that stopped him from embracing his unfakeable self.

Part of being in a toxic relationship with this 'blame others for the way you feel on the inside' impulsive persona is not accepting that every person sees the world in their own unique way, and you simply can't change that. In every session, Paul would ask me to work on clarifying a specific challenge and demystify the science of how the way he thinks creates the life events he so desperately wanted to change.

We also did work on his inner child, and diffused the emotional charges of people he resented the most by adjusting his perceptions. In doing so, he learnt to change the way he thought about situations that previously he would have felt deep hurt from, and he started to take back control of his feelings. Sometimes, when the situation he found himself in was too difficult to handle, instead of letting his OCD take over, he would keep reading 'A Path to Wisdom', and he chose to use the twenty-five mind engineering principles to defuse the destructive feelings and arouse a new dialogue in his mind that was in alignment with the clarity of the vision he created in one of our sessions together.

The more work we did with Paul to neutralise the one-sided emotions originating from many of his hurtful life experiences, the more in control and healthier he felt. Yes, on this journey, he experienced many doubts, fears and enemies, but he remained persistent and he was committed to healing and knowing himself. As many of his negative feelings, inner conflicts, and judgments of self and others disappeared, so did his epilepsy. In one of the sessions, I had tears of inspiration coming from my eyes as he shared how freeing and grateful he felt, as he no longer needed to take the epilepsy drugs he had been taking for over twenty years.

Just like Paul, many of you are prone to feeling the negativity from others, because you expect your friends, family, and work colleagues to change their ways. Often, your unrealistic expectations of others are what brings disillusionment, frustration and disappointment. When you have so many expectations from others, often you can misinterpret that as the cause for your depression, anxiety, and feelings of being out of control.

This expectation of chasing that which you can't have and seeking to avoid that which pains you is what feeds your depression and makes the situation much more severe. When depression takes over, you will find yourself making hasty major life decisions. Many depressed people I consulted suffered from an unnecessary sense of urgency and desperation about having to establish a special confidante or partner quickly.

Tremendous loneliness, separation, and rejection exists between people wearing similar distorted impulsive persona masks. It often shows up when you become intimately involved with someone. Why? because you expect this person to be always right and never wrong, always peaceful and never a warrior, always kind and never cruel, and so on. The more polarised you are, the more you end up attracting another individual who has the same issues you are avoiding seeing in yourself that show up in your life in an unseen form. It is up to you to use all you have learned so far to reveal the form in which it is showing up in your life, so that you can own it, love it, and transcend it.

So, start thinking about who you are and how you feel about things in your outer reality. This impulsive persona's façade constructed by a lifetime of crises can cause significant separation and ultimately impact your physical health. Being unfakeable is a vast quest to go through, as is the amount of times you must use the process required to identify the many versions of your wounded impulsive persona.

Go from Doing to Undoing

From the moment you are born, you start to create various layers of separation from the authentic being you came into this world to be. Each event that you had judged in one form or another becomes the bricks that build the walls that isolate the light and the power of your unfakeable individual in the prison of your creation.

You experience this type of existential loneliness and self-deception from birth, from the moment of separation from your mother. When your umbilical cord is cut, and you take your first breath in this physical dimension, you go through a drastic change in the environment in which you started your initial life, in your mother's womb.

Many of you as a baby, may have felt cared for, told what to think, do or not do, been shouted at or admired, loved or hated, held or put in a cot, smiled or frowned at, rejected or protected by your parents. As a child, you start to be moulded into a persona influenced by the injected values and programming that you received from your parents, culture, society, schools that you end up attending, and the environment in which you were born.

With the passing of time, you learn to forget who you are, forget to be curious, and to use the God-given power you came into this world with, and to embrace what is authentic about you. It is through this indoctrination process that you end up adopting a distorted impulsive persona born from the external factors mentioned. The playful qualities and the power to attract people with your free attitude towards life that you once had when you were babies becomes long forgotten.

You start to be different, separated and you learn to measure, compare, and judge your self-worth with others. You feel that you are not accepted if your views and the way you think is different or you end up feeling that you do not fit in the 'norm' forced upon you by others.

This long-lasting separation creates many bricks that lay the foundation of the mind's prison wall that stops you even being aware of the consequences that this forced indoctrination has in your adult life.

As teenagers, you start to explore the things that interest you, your sexual identity, the freedom to make your choices, and, most likely, you end up connecting with other teenagers who, like you have been brainwashed, and you learn to judge others who don't fit your model of reality. You learn to feel separated through being judgmental, made to feel guilty and shameful for listening to your wants and your needs completely ignoring your body's feelings and your emotional guidance system.

From not knowing and honouring your true authentic self, you start to live in the shadows of other people's light, afraid to let your authentic light shine. You see the world through other people's achievements, desires, and ultimately their values. It is this way of being that makes you give your power away. You learn to be subordinate to other people's wants and needs, and you start to be a people pleaser. At some point, you will begin to infatuate yourself with people whose values match your values and distance yourself from others who don't match your values.

As adults, you then go to university, you find a job, and you create another persona that you identify with, which once again separates you from your unfakeable self, the rest of your friends, your family and society.

Over time, from daily obeying this never-ending conditioning cycle, you lose control of your choices and you start to control others for as long as you can. From being consistent in your endeavours to control others, you learn to give your power away easily; and, the worst thing is, you may not even be fully aware of how you give your power away, which then puts you into situations where you feel controlled, or where others may feel controlled by you.

In hiding your real power behind this impulsive persona, you show to the world, that you continue to live your life by seeking validation from outside yourself. You demand valuation from the people you love and everyone you come into contact with.

Something to watch out for is a behaviour that we all do it from time to time, offering to help without ever being asked to deliver. You keep believing that it is all done in the name of love. And, if the other person says no, you label them as unappreciative.

Remaining unaware of your separated inner being, you let your false-self impulsive persona feed your narcissist side by naturally behaving this way. Your desire to be in control, influential, compelling and successful may also create even more inner anger, rejection, separation and resentment towards yourself and others.

This way of living can prevent you from being in the moment, in your heart, and with your soul. You may already know, that from being an active listener, and you can relate to from personal experience, that integrating our transient personas is a challenge on its own, and a massive hurdle to overcome.

Your unfakeability shows up in your life when you start to go from doing to undoing what you have learnt and so far known to be true in your life. Each time you experience a crash of the transient identity as you know it, you will give birth to a new character in the movie of your life. It is during this separation that most of you may feel the pain, but it is also where you can also grow the most.

It is, for this reason, that it is wise to consider seeking help from a coach, therapist, healer, or other qualified and trained professional who can provide the space for your transformations to happen. My clients' often share on social media how by taking them safely through the build and destroy process, that they experience the rise of the phoenix from the ashes of transformation; an essential process you need to undergo to live, love and lead a life authentically and freely on your terms.

Unfortunately, many people who seek my help, do so at the point when their pain or their problem is often too big to handle on their own, or it costs their business a lot of money, when they experience tremendous adversity that creates uncertainty in their lives, in their identity or their relationship crises, or the business challenges that comes from what's going on inside them.

Some of the common reasons many of my clients give when they book a consultation is the feeling of being anxious, depressed, lost in life, stressed, experiencing burnout, not having control of life situations and the direction their life is going. Others do it when they experience family conflicts, a relationship breaks up, job dissatisfaction, sudden career changes, financial issues, or they feel that their business is sinking, and that the livelihood of their employees or loved ones is threatened.

Please note, just like when your body is ill, taking preventive measures is wiser than reacting to circumstances at the moment. Thus, investing in upgrading your psychology as frequently as you consult your apps on your mobile phone can save you energy, money, pain and time.

It is up to you take back control of the situations you may find yourself in, invest in yourself and challenge yourself to grow before you start feeling lonely, exposed, or vulnerable. It is through consistently peeling back layer by layer, that you end up rebuilding a truthful and authentic identity.

Deep down, you know of the existence of the impulsive persona's façade through the feedback you receive through your body's ALARMs, your intuition, your gut feeling and the voice within that identifies whether your true authentic self is being expressed or not.

You also know it from listening to the voice of your spirit that is patiently awaiting you behind every masked persona that you show to the world. Each time you are not congruent in any of the critical areas of life, you are not being true to who your unfakeable being truly is – an encompassing individual that radiates gratitude and infuses the space and time with love and light. In being more unfakeable, you harmonise your relationship with your material and spirit nature. Only then, your spiritual intelligence, with its infinite qualities and abilities, expresses itself freely through your material self.

Each of the principles and their associated ideas you've learned so far is part of the mind's upgrading code that helps you to peel off the layers of your transient persona's false self-façade. It makes you durable so that you can face your fears, your self-deceptions and your worst nightmares with confidence. Practise them daily every time you need guidance, for they'll help you to embrace your inextricable individual.

Recollect the time when you learned something new, perhaps a new language, and you had to learn how to answer questions like:

What's your name? How old are you? Where do you come from? What is the name of your father, your mother? What interests you? Who do you want to be when you grow up? What song do you love the most?

Probably, at the time you were learning this, you didn't understand the complexity, difference or the real intention behind the questions. You just memorized the right answers. It was only later in life that you truly started to develop your analytical and emotional faculties, that suddenly those questions began to play a big part in the way others perceived you; and if what you said other's judged you for, you learnt to hide your true identity, and you started to undo some of the things you had learnt that no longer serve you.

The common ways most of you introduce yourself include your name, profession, relationship status, race, age, the religion you follow, the awards you have received or other descriptions. The truth is far from that; intuitively, you may already know or now have learned that the labels and the roles you currently identify yourself with are impermanent. They can disappear in the blink of an eye, change, and evolve.

You may lose your wife you once loved and end up calling yourself a widower, be fired from a job you once had and consider yourself to be redundant, or have an accident that impairs your beauty and now you find yourself feeling ugly. Just as every aspect of your physical self may vary through time, so can every element of the masked persona you may at this time show to the world you live in.

The truth of who you are is not derived from the transient persona's wants and needs, the limited self you have been conditioned to be, but the reality of your eternal existence your unfakeable individual knows. The only permanent thing about you is your awareness of you in any present moment.

It is your soul hidden somewhere in the corner, behind all of those transient identities that is the witness that non-judgmentally observes every action and every experience that you consciously or unconsciously create.

Before you continue your reading, here is an idea worth sharing with anyone you know who would benefit from a nugget of life-transforming wisdom:

Your soul is the only constant connection to all that life represents.

Your Life is an Expression of Your Consciousness

Unlike any other sentient being, you are capable of growing through self-reflection and consciously destroying and creating what's in your reality. The more you use what you are learning to go deeper, the more power the awareness of those two powerful forces are integrated into your authentic individual.

Acknowledge your desire to manifest unique experiences in alignment with your heart's calling in life, and this will keep you inspired to take daily actions that fulfil your authentic values and truth. Furthermore, spend time daily to observe your unfakeable self from a non-judgmental lens, and, in doing so, you will come to realize that your spirit without your body (matter) is expressionless, and that your body without the spirit is motionless.

The word Pneuma (πνεῦμα[1]) is an ancient Greek word for 'breath', and in a religious context for 'spirit' or 'soul'. It is why your spirit uses your physical body as a canvas in which it can express its freedom, creativity, and infinity.

It is why: **Your last breath is the final stroke your spirit makes in the painting of life.**

It is in honouring this truth of who you in your essence are and the wholeness of your being that can set you free, free from limiting beliefs, deceiving perceptions born out of judgements. It

---

[1] https://en.wikipedia.org/wiki/Pneuma

is your choice to acknowledge how all that you observe in others is also present in you. Recognising this in your life can help you to take back control of the direction that your life is going in for you to live authentically and with the freedom that your heart desires.

The next time you are challenged, use the shared exercises, ideas and principles to neutralise your emotions that are created from judgment. Honour your unfakeable being, its knowing, and the authentic power it has, and see how easy the path to abundance and expressing your highest version of yourself becomes.

The expectations of others to fit in within their value system and social norms may, unfortunately, cause you a lot of conflicts, discord and pain. But if you frequently self-reflect on your true desires and the life choices that make you feel lost, you can pave the path to consciously creating the freedom, success and the transformation you seek.

Living to satisfy your senses through an outside stimulus is what makes you live the illusion created by a false sense of self.

This illusion is what stops many of you from meeting your unfakeable you, honouring your truth, and growing your wealth and business exponentially. It is why Joel, the successful business owner of a technology company, started his life transformational coaching journey to help him grow his business. Deep down, he knew that not integrating these transient personas you are learning about into one authentic individual was the cause of all his disempowering behaviours, the acorn of the illnesses he had, and the toxic effects of the midlife crisis he found himself in.

On this journey to discover a buried truth, heal himself, and free his trapped soul that we co-created and described in 'Living My Illusion – The Truth Hurts' multi-award-winning documentary.

Both Joel, and later on, his wife Timea felt called upon to share with the world what my books, healing sessions, meditations, life and business consultations helped them accomplish. We put the documentary on Amazon Prime with a joint mission to raise awareness on the toxic effect the truth-twisting of our people-pleasing, and self-deceptive transient personas have on our business, professional, and personal lives.

One of the common misconceptions I see that sometimes people hold onto as they learn the of importance of living in accordance with their higher priority of values is to use what they've learned as a justification not to practise what they now perceive as low priority actions. This way of behaving is what keeps many of you in a self-justification loop that acts as a disservice to your growth and further fuels your self-deceptive ego persona.

It is wise to re-wire your brain to reveal how by doing low priority actions, you can build the wealth and the reality whereby you can pay others to take such actions for you. It is in maintaining this required harmony between the high and the low priority value actions that can help you to achieve great results and bring more fulfilment and inner peace to all of your life's experiences.

If you don't, you'll waste time trying to ease the suffering and the loss of energy associated with your self-deceptive animal behaviour driven persona that wants pleasure without pain. You'll end up in a self-destructive cycle of questioning your past and blaming others for not getting what your one-sided ego persona wants; and, you'll rarely stop to look at your self-destructive behaviours that do not unmask the illusion conceived by your self-deceptive nature disguised as, "I am not doing so and so, as it is not in alignment with my highest-values."

Every time I helped clients create instant procrastination breakthroughs that came about due to my assisting them in creating clarity of their authentic values, and teaching them how to harmonise low and high-priority actions in a way that supports their top seven authentic values.

You may think your genetics influences your experiences of life. That may be true to a degree, but there is growing scientific evidence on how your actions, attitudes, and perceptions of your surrounding environment play a much larger part in gene expression and in shaping your reality. Remain flexible and adaptable enough to make the most of what you are learning throughout this book, as it will awaken in you more choices and possibilities for growth, freedom, and meaning than you realize. While experiencing moments of feeling unloved, uncared for, and unworthy may be inevitable, suffering is always optional.

To start living authentically is to accept how the 100% unfakeable you is 50% Ying and 50% Yang, 50% bad and 50% good, 50% kind and 50% cruel, 50% dumb and 50% smart, etc. To honour the voice of your calling desires, and your intention must be to put the values that this voice represents high on the list of the priority of your values. And, to daily take actions in alignment to your true calling in life.

Before you move on to principle number five, make sure that you spend some time to complete the exercise below so that you can uncover your triggers of giving your power away, of what needs changing, and what painful parts need healing. Some of the questions below might cause other issues to surface. Write down what comes up for you in as much details as you can, and give it a voice. Pay attention to that voice, as it is what your body is trying to communicate to you and through you.

Probably, you will hear what comes up for you for a reason; to uncover projected unmet expectations, and to recognize the factors that may be generating a one-sided perception, and ultimately bring about feelings of not being in control.

Being unfakeable isn't easy, but if you are game, next time you encounter problematic people and situations, use what you have learnt so far in order to see them objectively as they are and not as you want them to be.

Before you go to the next chapter, do the following exercise:

- Think about the most relevant event, situation, or person who you may have had an argument with, or who you feel emotionally charged towards.
- Go within, calm your mind, and let your unfakeable self-non-judgmentally observe the situation, the event, or the unlovable person you just thought about, until you see the wholeness of whatever you perceive as one-sided. Once you truly understand how for every judgment there is an associated benefit to you, your heart opens and you'll experience tears of gratitude.

Open your eyes, take a pen and paper, or open a word document and on a piece of paper, answer the following questions:

- How do you currently describe yourself to others?
- What did your parents tell you about you in your early childhood?
- What kind of child were you?
- Were you outgoing or shy, funny, a troublemaker?
- What toys did you play with?
- What activities did you repeat?
- What did you dream about the most?
- What things did you dislike and like about yourself?
- What situations trigger anger, resentments, and other ego states to come out?
- What makes you nervous, and why?
- In what environment do you feel safe and relaxed?
- When you do things, why do you do them?
- What's your greatest fear? How does this fear affect your decisions?

- Where are you most comfortable? Is it at work, with your family at home, with your friends, or outside in nature?
- What upsets or angers you?
- What is your inspiration for taking action?
- What would you do otherwise in your life if you pressed the reset button and were able to start your life over again?
- What better choices would you make going forward?
- How would your life be different from the one you are currently living right now?
- Is there something that brings you joy? Are you seeking validation and approval? Or, maybe you're feeling guilty or under pressure?
- If you were to tell the truth about yourself to others (for a job interview or a romantic interest or in social gatherings), what would you say?
- Assume you are safe, and you have all your basic needs met. How would you act then?
- Assuming everyone loves and appreciates you for being unfakeable, how would you then describe yourself to others?
- If you strip all the above labels away, who are you then? What is your truth?

In completing the exercise above, you'll raise your awareness of how both those who challenge and support you help you to know your authentic being a bit better. Don't forget to ask yourself: Is there something else here, if I am reacting to an outside stimulus or bad behaviour, that I still judge?

Create an action list in alignment with your vision, mission and purpose in life. Daily do the actions, as that step will move you closer to taking back control, to growing your worth, and to live life authentically and freely on your terms.

If you get emotional and have negative thoughts as you go through this process, your dis-inspired ego is standing in your way. Keep digging, and keep writing down whatever is challenging you, in the knowledge that it is also supporting you. We all have a dark side, but, remember, it is only a part of you and not the whole you.

Your innermost truth is there to guide you on the path that brings you to a place of acknowledgement, balance and a flow of love. As you go through this process, you will reach a place within yourself where you acknowledge that in essence, you are free, intelligent and interconnected being made of light and love.

Use your answers to self-reflect. Pause to ask what's underneath, that is preventing you from giving your power away, and what actions you can take to own your power. In doing an objective analysis of yourself, you will learn to act like a consultant or a self-detective, and you become your own coach who objectively analyses every response and situation, using facts and real data.

If you catch yourself thinking or telling others: "My manager yells and does not listen." Stop, go back, keep digging, and use the questions and the principles you are learning, to self-analyse more. It will help you to transform your negative inner dialogue about what a jerk your partner, your friends, your family or your senior managers are. In owning what you see in others, you become more objective and more radiant.

This way of observing life with objectivity can make you more energetic, fashionable, and productive at work and in life.

The more detailed you are in your answers above, the more the need to win dissipates, the more in control you will feel. In personal relationships, this need to 'win' even when you know you are 'wrong' doesn't benefit anyone. It just leaves you both feeling bad. If that is your intention, you'd better go and watch a play in the theatre or play an impulsive control game on your Xbox.

Next time someone pushes your emotional trigger button, and you don't have the time to do all the exercises and answer all of the questions above, here is a calming and neutralising practice that you can do.

Close your eyes, take a few deep breaths in and out, focus on your heart and bring this person into your mind's eye (third eye). With your eyes closed, bring your focus directly into the centre of their eyes and silently say the following mantra:

I am you. You are me, and together we are unfakeable as one. I am you. You are me, and together we are love!

Keep repeating this mantra until your unfakeable identity is at ease with all that is, and you will have tears of inspiration in your eyes that will be trickling down your face.

Master the Virtue of Loving Prudently

Principle #5:
Choose Love as Your Military Commander that Wins Every Battle in Life

Congratulations on making it this far on our journey together. I bet, many of you are extremely curious to learn more about how principle five can help you to master the virtue of loving prudently.

Often many of you will find yourself asking the question: "What creates the resistance you feel between your mind, your heart, and your soul?" It is the judgment that becomes the wind that blows out the candlelight burning in the lamp of your unfakeable grateful heart. What helps you get rid of this resistance is filtering your reality through the lens of objectivity, which in turn, calms your mind storms created by your one-sided perceptions. And, in this state of inner calm, you can listen to your heart's infinite wisdom and unleash the healing power of love.

So, you may be asking yourself, "How do I then eliminate judgment from my life, so eternal light shines in the seat of my soul, my heart?" Well, you can't. It is just one of the many traits you have. What you can do, is give rise to your authentic, unfakeable self, that embraces judgment as part of its wholeness intelligently.

It's often said that love is what makes us a better person, it can heal us, and move mountains. However, life itself, with its hardships teaches us that the same love can also divide us, make us jealous, and turn us against one another. A good testament of this is many of the most significant wars that started in the name of love, and what's very interesting, many of those wars also ended in the name of love.

To learn about peeling off the tough love façade you've built throughout your life to love prudently is a life's journey. As you go through every paragraph of this chapter, make it your intention to know the beneficial role of your transient tough love persona through the dynamics of an intimate relationship.

Sharing your life with another person can turn into a permanent struggle as you cope with your fears, control mechanisms, and the rigid beliefs coming alive every time you are being challenged. It is this fierce love warrior that your tough love persona uses that impedes your ability to love nonjudgmentally and unconditionally.

Like it or not, being in a marriage or in a relationship with another person, you open up parts of yourself that you don't show to anyone until your guard is down; those disowned parts of you that are typically found deep inside your subconscious mind where you store most of what happens to you.

The reason most of you feel that you grew apart after being with someone for a while, is because of the one-sided expectation you have around what love is, and what it is not. As a result, often the many hurts that are hidden behind each other's tough love persona are overlooked in the 'blossoming' stage of the relationship. During which, your hormones and your infatuation with each other take over.

During this stage in your relationship, if not careful, your infatuation for each other makes you blind. You fail to see the dangers that come from not knowing about your tough love persona mask. It's your blindness to your downsides that prevents you from seeing them in the person you started to date, are in a relationship with or may have married. It is this that makes many of you perceive that you've fallen in love with that person blindly.

Like it or not, at some point in the relationship, the more time you spend with each other, the more you start to see in one another the blind spots, the tough love persona's façade that you don't usually show to others. Thus, being in a relationship, it is an excellent opportunity to discover your masked tough love persona's disowned parts, and grow the most. That said, both parties need to be willing to go through this unpeeling, revealing, and transformational process that can increase the feeling of love you have for one another, for the long term.

The truth is, to love prudently depends a lot on your willingness to take off the mask. To face the little lies, desires, and secrets, that you keep away from the person you love. To reveal to each other openly the shameful things you may have done that you because of the fear of losing one another are afraid to disclose. To share the guilt, you may be carrying from a traumatic event that you mask and use, is to hide the truth.

Know this; it's impossible to get to know someone straight away, and often it takes a lifetime. Even then, you still may discover things about that person you never knew. This reminds me of the love lesson I learned from my mother, Ljutvije Selimi, at the age of sixteen. Having dated many girls, I finally found a girl I was head over heels in love with. Her name was Besa, a beautiful girl with long curly black hair, a gorgeous face, fit physical body, thin lips, and most importantly, she was the daughter of a reputable doctor my parents approved off.

In the beginning, everything was excellent and beautiful, but as time went on, I started to realize that she was not the perfect girl I had imagined. When it all came to an end, I went home to tell my mother, this was it for me, I no longer wanted to live, and without love, I might as well commit suicide.

My mother, stubborn, strong and strict, yet at the same time extraordinarily loving and a wise woman, sat me down and said to me, "Son, you see this expensive crystal glass?"

I said, "Yes."

She then said, "With your father Shaqir, we bought the crystal set it belongs to at a costly shop, and we have worked very hard for many years to save the money required to purchase it and make our home as beautiful as it is."

She then took one of the crystal glasses. She threw it far away from harm, on the marble floors of our garden, where it smashed into tiny pieces.

She took my hand and said, "Son, let's walk over there." As we approached the place where the glass had landed, she said, "Son, is there any more value in the crystal glass I just broke?"

I said, "No, Mum."

She then continued, "If I asked you to put the broken pieces together, do you think you could do it in a way that would bring the glass back as it was?"

I immediately said, "No Mum, there will be many pieces missing and it won't look the same."

"Do you believe we now have the money to replace the glass I just broke?"

I said, "Yes, Mum, we have plenty of money to buy anything we want, but can money buy me love?" I asked.

At that moment, she sat next to me, and with her deep sky blue, bright eyes on me, she lovingly said,

"Money can buy you many things, including people who you may think love you; but, no matter how hard you try, you can't mend a broken relationship that was based

on infatuation and satisfying the needs of your senses. One day, the true love I have for you will find you."

So, smile at me, say thank you that it ended, and remember this moment for life. It will guide you in finding your true love.

As I hugged her, with tears running down my cheeks, she said, "My dear son, it took your father and me ten years to prudently love one another, you have a lifetime ahead of you to find the person who stays with you and beside you, through thick and thin."

Since that moment, I have been on a quest to find my true love. I have dated many people, and each one taught me things about myself, that I never knew. Though deep down, I know that one day, the person who I love and am loved by, just like my mother will not be captivated by how I look, the number of degrees I have completed, and what titles of authority I have been given. But, it will be someone with whom I can spend a lifetime discovering each other's vulnerabilities and greatness; and on this authenticity seeking journey to owning my wounded tough love persona, true love found me and if you let it, it can find you.

Demystify Your Idea of What Love Should be, Must be, and is

Like the other transient personas you read about in the previous chapters, your tough love persona is built from every dating and relationship experience you've ever had; including early childhood events when you learnt what love is and what it is not from the people closest to you-often being your parents, grandparents, brothers, sisters, friends and the societal norms you grew up in.

Many life adversities you may have had as well as the one you may have observed in your parents and people closest to you have influenced you in what you believe love is and what expectations are attached to allowing yourself to be loved.

For instance, if from an early age, you were told that you must do everything to keep your relationship together; if you are not careful, this belief may force you to remain in an abusive relationship. The worst thing is that you may even believe it's your fault. Therefore, feel damaged, guilty and weak enough to walk away.

Being in a toxic relationship makes you feel alone, abandoned, rejected, unworthy, and unloved. Yet, despite your body's ALARM's feedback on what you need to do, you don't listen, and you continue to remain a victim of that relationship in the name of what love means to you.

In this situation, the seeds of the lack of self-love, self-worth, and non-acceptance creates a void within you that drives you to build the self-made fortress where no one is good enough to love you.

I often observe this tough love persona's façade coming out in many of the consultation sessions with clients who seek to find true love, 'fix' their broken relationship, or divorce their spouses. Some ask me to heal their broken heart, teach them how to best address arguments, conflicts, and fears, and others to help them to ease the pain of being sexually rejected. In the pursuit to attract their ideal partner so that they can feel 'whole' again, many of them deep down wanted to get to the bottom of what caused the relationship issues that they found themselves in.

If this is you, you can either get an expert to help you, or you can start with having clarity of what your actual authentic values are, and by identifying what disempowering beliefs or behaviours are stopping you from finding or being in a love-infused relationship. Depending on your circumstances, you can either decide to improve the relationship you are in or decide it's time to move on and break up.

This was the case with Susan, a career-driven senior executive in her mid-30s, working for one of the Fortune 500 companies in the city of London, who started to consult with me to help her find a co-loving partner to build a family with. On this relationship coaching journey together, she began to see how the reality she found herself in did not match with what she thought her values and beliefs were.

As I started to question her on what a loving relationship is and is not, she realized that the relationship values she had reflected the voice of her mother more than what she truly wanted for herself. Deep down, what love meant to her was what she had observed in her parents, concerning what love is, should be and must be.

This realization made her dig deeper, and as we looked for more events to analyse her tough love persona, she saw with clarity that she was pursuing a one-sided expectation from the man who would eventually end up being her husband. This illusion was keeping her away from love finding her. It was this false awareness of what love is, that made her unconsciously go for men who her parents would approve of, but which would not necessarily be the right partner for her.

Once we clarified her values and created clear action steps to put being in a co-loving relationship on her top ten priority list of importance, she started to date guys that she enjoyed being with. We worked on many levels to upgrade her mind's codes for the relationship she wanted, from creating a clear vision for her future, owning traits she judged outwardly, to creating a clear mental picture of how she wanted to be loved and love, prudently.

A year down the line, I was at Sue's, and Tom's wedding in Spain, celebrating two authentic individuals whose vows to each other were the words I taught them in one of our relationship breakthrough sessions:

I am what you are, and you are what I am. Together, we are unfakeably in love.

The above mantra was based on a mantra I created in the autumn of 1990, when, due to the atrocities of the civil war, I found myself homeless and sleeping rough on the streets of London, with no one to love or be loved by. It was the **"I am what you are, and together we are love"** mantra I recited over and over until I fell asleep to help me to forgive those who had harmed me and those I loved the most.

Remember, the actual fuel that generates the inner discord that creates the pain is not the person you are dating; it is an unnoticed pain that you are not listening to. The hurt you develop over a lifetime from the countless arguments, the unrealistic expectations of self and others, and the tensions with people you love and have been loved the most. Usually, it is with your parents, grandparents, family members, people you dated, married, or adopted you. And for some of you, later on in life from your children and your friends too.

If your perception of the relationship with your parents in early childhood was a difficult one, the hurt child, at some point in your adult life, when you are seeking your real love, will interfere and stop you from loving prudently. Sometimes without even being aware of your behaviours, you unsocially, will want to control and seek validation from the person you want in your life. And at other times, some of you may even withhold love as a way of punishing others who you feel may have played a role in hurting you in some way. This toxic, vicious behaviour of your tough love persona is not just typical in relationships, it also presents itself at work, with colleagues, teams, family members, and close friends without you even realizing it.

Let's say you have a friend or an acquaintance that you have spent a lot of time with, and for some reason you stop seeing them regularly. You keep telling them via text or social media that you love them and you appreciate them, although you don't call them to hear their voice, you don't make time to see them, and every time they get in touch with you, you make all kinds of excuse, such as how busy you are.

However, your unfakeable being knows that you are being untruthful, fake, and are pursuing actions that are not aligned to the prudent love your unfakeable individual is capable of giving. Yet, you let your tough love persona's actions tell a different story about you.

Instead of letting this person know the truth of not wanting them to be a part of your life, you give in to the illusion of punishing them by withdrawing your love. When circumstances bring you together, you then come up with all kinds of excuses why you have not seen them for such a long time. You bring out your tough love persona façade and you tell them how busy you are. Before you know it, the friend that was once always there for you, the one who loved and supported you through thin and thick, suddenly becomes a distant stranger, unworthy of your love. Letting your tough love persona get away with any excuses you can think of to justify your inactions and actions can destroy what you value the most in your life, to love and to be loved prudently.

If in those moments of dishonesty, you look within, and you will notice how the lack of self-love, self-care and understanding has power over your unfakeable being that in its essence is loving. It is in those moments of significant separation from your true authentic self and the world around you, that your intuition can wake you up and make you break through that illusion. The undesired situation you may find yourself in is simply your unfakeable self's way of awakening your greatness, love, and power.

Many of you feel that falling in love is a plan you must create and follow. The truth is far from that, without you even being aware of it, it happens. You suddenly find yourself falling in love with a person who mobilizes in you your most profound conflicts, all that has remained unsolved in your personal history. These conflicts may lead to you having a tensioned relationship but, if both parties are committed, have an unexplainable bond, and are willing to grow together, it is in the very complicated relationship, that you'll see through each other's tough love persona's façades, heal your wounds and learn to love prudently. As my late mum Ljutvije would say, "Love, will find you, and it will be where you least expect it to be."

All of us develop a social personality. Within the relationship, your sentimental nature is involved, which is mostly unseen in society. Rational connections with others help you solve social issues but may not necessarily solve your love issues in an intimate relationship with each other. In many of the couples I have assisted, I observe how a lack of social life, fear and distrust, one-sided expectations and an unbalanced masculine and feminine dynamic, can make the couple unstable or conflictive.

In your childhood, you may start to believe that you are not worthy of being loved as you are. Then you force your unfakeable self to create a persona matching that which your parents want from you.

It is in observing your tough love persona that you discover worthiness, self-love, and the art of self-acceptance. The great way to make a breakthrough in your love life is through a non-judgmental view of one another; whether being with someone you want to date, are dating, or are in an intimate relationship with, or who is simply a friend or someone who is closest to you.

In holding a non-judgmental view of the other person you've been having a relationship with you can quickly realize why they pretend to be or show themselves to be a tough love persona, and thus do not deserve to be loved. As you learn to observe yourself non-judgmentally, you start to remove the tough love persona's facade you show to the world. In doing so, you cast away from yourself the desire of always fitting a particular model of loving or being loved. You simply learn to sit with your entire authentic being, listen to it, and let it express love freely.

Creating moments of genuine surrender and frankness in relationships will reward you with the discovery that you can be loved as you are, without the deceptions and the expectations of your tough love persona. The greatest love is possible, and the reason you know this is because of moments in your life when you are loved as you are, for who you are, without the need to change.

Concealing your true nature in the name of love is something that you have learned to do from the moment you were born. You are validated for the good things you do, and you are punished for the bad things you do. You develop a skewed perception of what love is, hiding your true self from the many fears that have enveloped your being since a very young age.

The fear of rejection, not being good enough, not being successful, not being good looking enough, not being loud or confident enough, or not worthy of love, is what scares you. It makes you vulnerable, and of course, it makes you not wanting to accept this. Your warrior tough love persona uses your vulnerability as building blocks for the tough love façade that you show to the world. To prevent you from genuinely surrendering, seeing the truth of what love truly is, and, ultimately, leading you on a path to suffering.

Emotional co-dependence makes you vulnerable, and it makes you so resistant to the pains of your relationship that you stopped listening to it a long time ago. In shutting down your 'feeling challenged is not what love is', you awaken the awareness that love is both pain and pleasure in equal proportions, and that both challenge and support serve you in equal measures.

Going on a journey to peel off the warrior tough love persona's façade, you come to accept that pain is an inevitable part of this journey, but you acknowledge that suffering is optional. You chose to observe your unfakeable, authentic self objectively, and, in doing so, you opened your heart and you let love flow freely and unconditionally.

To let suffering take over your being is neurotic. It makes you not accept that pain is serving you. Instead, it forces you to do 'something' to eliminate it. You switch partners, and you blame the society, your work colleagues, family and friends, parents, the person you are with, and so on. Guaranteed, neither of these behaviours is helpful on your journey to find your true love, they will just keep you hooked up to therapy, addictions and segregated, alone in the wretched caves of solitude.

Before you continue your reading, here is an idea worth remembering and sharing:

Pain and pleasure are the battery and the light of the torch that illuminates the path for love to find you.

When Judgment Goes, Love Appears

Acceptance that the answers you are seeking are within you happens when you turn your entire focus towards finding solutions to life's adversities becomes to look within with objectively. It is only then that you come to that place of tranquillity, acceptance, inner peace, freedom and prudential love you may be seeking.

Often at the beginning of some of my client's transformational coaching journey, they cannot accept the possibility that the real source of relationship conflicts is within themselves. Frequently, couples who don't go through the relationship coaching process, who don't seek help from a trained professional, either stay in an abusive relationship or they end it badly. Some people continue to recreate the illusion of a one-sided tough love persona in another relationship. When they no longer feel that they can control the other person, they leave the person and simply turn their backs on ever falling in love, thus avoiding having to acknowledge that whatever they dislike in the partner also exists in them. Failing to truly recognise the duality existing in love relationships is also present in every person they date.

Many of you may prefer to believe that the problem was with the other person or precisely within the relationship you had, without asking a simple question:

Why am I in this situation? What is my contribution to creating the hardships I am experiencing in this relationship? What traits am I judging that I have disowned? What masked personas am I giving voice to in this relationship? What lessons are my unfakeable being learning by being in this experience? What unlovable, traits in me are screaming for my love?

The reason many of you find it hard to solve your problems that become relationship issues is because of judgments coming from your addiction to one-sided psychology. In the field of psychology, many would describe it as the 'hurt of the wounded ego or the wounded inner child.' This hurt child is in all of us, you carry it inside of you, and it stirs feelings of anger in you every time you don't listen to the truth of your authentic, unfakeable self. This is because of the criticism you've received and the pain resistance you have built inside yourself since birth. You are now unloading freely in your intimate relationships and in your close friendships the pain that you were not able to express in your childhood.

My client Sue, who I mentioned earlier on, at some point during our relationship coaching journey together, realized the importance that her critical and wounded inner child played in her experience of love. I recollect how each session focused on healing her inner child, she would find it hard to open the communication channel required for her to listen to her inner child's pain and pleasures.

Initially, she found the idea of communicating with her inner child ridiculous and very challenging. As we examined her behaviours through every relationship she had been through, she started to go deeper within, and at some point, her inner child's voice spoke to her. She finally understood her inner child's deep loneliness that she had experienced as a result of years of criticism and neglect.

She saw how the abandonment she had received from the various men she had dated was helping her to realize the importance of healing her inner child and becoming emotionally available and mentally ready to love freely on her terms. The more healing work we did on her inner child, the more her inner child started to come out to play, the more she saw what lived behind the tough love façade that had isolated her inner child.

In one of our sessions, I took her through a guided meditation that brought her and her inner child to play together in an oasis of unconditional love. She described how in this place she and her inner child were free to play with one another, express each other's feelings, and harness the infinite love existing between her and her inner child.

After she opened her eyes up, she said to me, "Tony. You brought me to experience the healing power of love you always talk about. I felt my inner child, and I was at one with it."

It is in this non-judgmental state of being that love magically appears in your life. Adopting a non-judgmental point of view can heal your relationship with your inner child and puts you in a position to awaken the healing powers of your unfakeable authenticity, gratitude and prudential love.

If your partner lashes out and unloads their pains on you, you can choose to engage with your pain, or be a clean mirror from which he or she can self-reflect and heal. Instead of fighting, reacting or responding from your tough love persona's pain, you can alternatively ask yourself what the connection of what the other person is experiencing with your personal history is. What things have you not yet managed to solve that preceded your relationship?

There are many of you who, no matter how many people around you love you, deep down, you always feel abandoned, disrespected, rejected, and unloved by others. This is an excellent opportunity for you to realize your possessiveness, your inner child pain, and the protective mechanisms of the many masked personalities that you may have developed that are marked by your childhood traumas.

Never underestimate the value in investing in a trained specialist, a coach, therapist, healer, or a psychologist to show you how to integrate those personas into the authentic individual you know you are. They are a great resource to help you revise that personal sensation of abandonment, loneliness, and fear of being rejected into all that your unfakeable individual is. Any short term investment you do to help you to be in a co-loving relationship will pay off in the long run, by saving you a lot of emotions, frustrations, money, stress and in time-your most precious asset.

To understand how experiences beyond the relationship you may currently be in, actualizes presently in your life as an old pain sensation, see if you can track moments in your memory when you felt the same inner discord. There are plenty of exercises throughout the book that can help you do that. Use them daily to upgrade your caveman psychology and to enhance your relationship.

Not taking full responsibility for your life just leads to blaming others and perpetuating your pain and suffering. As you use what you have learned so far to peel off this tough love persona's façade, you learn to stop looking outwardly to find a person to blame for the pain felt inward.

Instead, when challenged, you go within yourself, and you become humbled and grateful for the other person's role of being the mirror you need at that moment, to love the unlovable in you and unleash your authentic power; this God-given power that is trapped behind the gates protected by your wounded fierce warrior tough love persona that are waiting to be opened to release the power behind them.

The other issues that get unveiled by choosing to peel your tough love persona's façade aside are; reasons, resistance and resignation. They are the difference between acceptance of what should be and what is.

Departure involves suffering because of the idea that things could be better for you. Acceptance means assuming that something cannot be different, but your attitude and your perceptions can be changed by observing the situation nonjudgmentally. This will increase your ability to care for one another lovingly.

Resignation involves the idea of an injustice ('this should not have happened to me') that the subject or the partner failed you in something. What usually follows is constant complaints, criticism and harsh judgment that accompanies you throughout life and in every situation. This drains your life force. It is what creates what you label as 'the energy vampires' that for an unbeknown reason you easily attract into your life, despite desperately wanting to avoid them.

All of the many layers of the idealized image you have of the transient personas you are learning about prevent you from unleashing the authentic power of your unfakeable self. The power you have hidden away in the caves of wretched solitude, from the fear of what may happen if you live to your true potential, which is, infinite. Not being aware of this inner separation, you'll continually try to fit in already established relationship models or fail to rise to the standard of untouchable relationship ideals.

The authentic unconditioned love that you seek first and foremost needs to be present in you. In loving your unfakeable self, you love other people solely for who they are, as they are, and what they are. Thus, to love prudently is to master the art of taming the light and the dark God-like forces of your unfakeable, authentic being.

It is in honouring your dual nature that you can balance your perceptions of who you are, who the other person is, and then you can let each other's authenticity strengthen the love you have for one another.

Integrating your tough love persona into your authentic, unfakeable self is an enriching experience your future self will thank you for. Do this integration process as part of your daily living with your partner, date, or even a friend or a family member who will be conscious of this inner battle and willingly engage with you. When you are trying to do this in a relationship where one of the partners has no interest at all, your partner may see you as being controlling, critical, and pushy, which becomes counterproductive as it forces them to close their emotional pathways off from you.

A physical wound requires medicine and time to heal. Similarly, for your old heart wounds to heal, they need the five principles, and they need you to invest the necessary time to upgrade your psychology. I've taken many people through the process you are learning, safely, and through specific questioning I'll be able to help you to express pent up rage and pain authentically and freely. That way, you can ensure that your partner does not feel that they are the only receiver of these reactions.

One thing you can do to start breaking this tough love persona's façade is to determine the origin of the fears that open the door behind which your rage lives and what lets it loose. The transformation must be real, not induced by will or wishful thinking. Moments of anger and frustration only cause pain, as the person discovers that the reality is not how they had envisioned it.

Another way for you to recognize that you are wearing this tough love persona's façade is to notice when you fail to listen. Not knowing how to truly listen and hear each other is what sits at the root of inadequate communication. If there is no transparent, two way, mindful and trustworthy communication, then there is no connection between the two of you. You end up feeling that you are not being listened to, and this, in turn, makes you feel alone in that relationship.

If the other person you may be with is angry, in just a blink of an eye, you may think that you have done something wrong and, what's worse, that you have to do something to make the other party not feel angry anymore. I have observed this controlling attitude clients display when I fire questions at them that are designed to diffuse relationship conflicts; as well as in people I know in my private and social life. In a situation like this, if you feel that you may have done something wrong, you might stand aloof and refuse to listen to your partner. Often that is the case with women who think they are not being heard by men. Unlike most men, women more naturally express emotions and are usually not even asking for something to be done, but simply to be listened to.

Let's face it, we as men are problem solvers, solution-driven beings, and we love to take care of the people we love by providing for them. Women, on the other hand, are different. Perhaps the only thing they want from a man is to feel wanted, to be listened to, and to be appreciated for the nurturing they bring into our lives.

However, in today's world where a man is expected to be both emotionally intelligent and masculine, often most people out there forget one historical fact that men were 'built' for action, to fight and to provide for the family, to keep them safe and not for having emotional strength. Despite the fantastic work many man have done on themselves, to bridge that gap, unfortunately for many men, to be sensitive is a sign of weakness, femininity, and a huge hurdle to overcome.

Most men unconsciously believe that a woman telling them something is asking for their help. Moreover, they think that if they can't solve the woman's problem, then they must be failing. That's why many men don't even bother to listen in most cases. They just switch on their 'do' mode. This dynamic is not exclusive to male or female heterosexual relationships; it is equally visible and recognisable in same-sex couples when the healthy masculine and divine feminine energies are out of balance.

Pay attention to this, as these kinds of challenges, dynamics, and obstacles arising from stigma are present in any relationship you create in your life whether it be with people who you date, friends, family members, with work colleagues, clients, or in business.

In being more of your authentic self, you can easily shed the layers built from pain and one-sided perceptions and start to own your disowned parts of your unfakeable individual. It is your authentic self that acknowledges the role your worst and best parts play in your relationship with yourself, those you love, and in everyone around you.

Being your authentic self is the recipe for becoming more present, a better listener, and diminishes your need to control and compete with one another. You begin to avoid chipping in with your two cents, judging or attempting to change anything about the other person. You learn to hear each other's personal history, and let it acknowledge the role it played in knowing the duality of each other's nature. It is this kind of awareness where ones perceived unlovable differences become what awakens the love that unites you in each other's uniqueness. This is the co-loving, co-nurturing, and co-creating relationship that many of you are seeking.

Love finds its way to you as you break the single expectation of self and other illusions your masked personas create, and as you undo what you have learned to be 'fake news' about you, you can then shower the duality of your nature with the light of your wholeness that you already know exists in you and in everything that your senses observe.

You may be eager to know what the glue is that holds these masks firmly attached to you, that is so hard to remove, and is invisible. Let me satisfy your curiosity; it is called judgment, fuelled by the lack of internal emotional control and denying the particle behaviours that exist at the micro-level that are also present at the macro-level.

You grew up being surrounded by people who use criticism, expectations, and judgment to get you to do what they want you to do. Unbeknown to you, your mind was trained to conform to other people's desires, ideas and wishes for you. It's what created the masked personas that you are now masterfully learning to integrate into your authentic individual who has the power to bend reality.

In Letting Go, You Let Love in

What controls you is often present in every area of your life, although frequently what controls you is unnoticed by you because you are used to it. In the absence of having self-worth, you may resort to psychological tactics that play on other people's insecurities to convince yourself that you've gained control over them falsely.

To best illustrate why in letting control go you let love in, I am going to share with you a short story of my client James. A wealthy serial entrepreneur, father of two children, and a devoted husband who after seeing a client video on my YouTube channel sought my help to address relationship issues that put him on a path to addiction, burnout, and loss of productivity at work and in the bedroom.

For the first coaching session, I arranged for him to meet me at the Grosvenor Hotel by Victoria station. Shortly after I had started to take him through the initial consultation process his phone rang, and rang, and rang. I saw the name of the caller displayed on his phone. It was his wife who we were just talking about. I said to him it might be urgent, feel free to pick up. Instead, he smugly said no it is not and he declined the call.

There was a period of silence, and then he went on to say, "Gotta' let her work for it. You know what I mean."

I looked straight into his sky-blue eyes, and I said, "James, no, I don't. Care to explain?"

He went on to say, "Tony, the more I ignore my wife, the more she calls me, and if my marriage was to last, I have to make her know that without me she can't do what she wants. This way, I can make sure she keeps calling me every day to ask for what she needs, so we remain together forever."

Through further questioning, we got to the bottom of the same behaviour that made her partner furious as she rejected him when he would come home, feeling hopeless, unwanted and tired.

The reason he believed that this was the best way to keep his marriage together while he worked hard to provide for the family was that his father did the same to keep his mum who always used to say to his father, "One day when my children grow up, I am leaving you." And, when he, his brothers and his sisters grew up, his mum left his father, and he ended up dying alone in a care home.

As we continued with our sessions, he came to understand how the behaviours that caused the most pain was his animalistic and amygdala fear-driven responses. I took a brain diagram and I explained to him the function of the amygdala, and how by engaging with his animal instinct, he was chasing that which he felt he could conquer. He was running away from what he felt could defeat him. In each consultation, he started to share how there were many other incidents that he could relate to this pain and pleasure-seeking behaviour.

I recollect saying to him, "There's the rub. If you start a relationship with fear and control games and you build a foundation for love based on psychological manipulation and mind control, at what point in your life will you decide to stop it?"

Two years passed by fast. During the sessions, James started to become better at seeing the unhidden motives of his undesired behaviours. He used the principles we shared to change the way he thought about the relationship with himself, his wife, and with everyone else at work. His unfakeable being started to realise what love is, intuitively, and what it is not. The deeper he went within, the more self-realizations he was experiencing. At some point on our journey together, I got him to draw parallels to show how the way he was with his wife was a mirror reflection of how his father had been with his mum, and how the same motives created the behaviours he asked me to change with his work colleagues, the people he hung out with socially after work. The harsh environment he grew up in made him program himself to be the tough guy who appears to have everything and everyone under his control.

The less judgmental he became, the less disempowering beliefs and one-sided opinions of self and others he started to have, the more he felt there was no longer such a need to control situations, his wife, and the people he managed. He would tell me how after each session that he would go home and share with his wife all the lessons he was learning, how in being vulnerable, he was learning to love himself and appreciate his wife more. Once, he also sent me an e-mail about an article he had written in his company's intranet openly sharing the importance of being adaptable, being open to learning, and showing his vulnerability with people he did not know played a crucial role in giving rise to his becoming a true authentic leader.

At one of our sessions, with tears in his eyes, he said, "Tony, I just want to say I love and appreciate you. You have transformed my mind on so many levels. I never thought that I could let go of my deep-felt fear of losing my wife, my income, and my kids. You truly set me free. Thank you."

While most people get into a relationship to attain a sense of security and true love, James's strategy was to keep his wife feeling fearful and insecure about herself. His tactics were fuelled by his internalised fears and the only way he thought he could keep his wife was through controlling her choices, injecting fear by threatening to leave her, not providing for the kids and taking advantage of her kind heart. It took him some time after our first coaching session to finally break free from the controls of his warrior tough love persona that had been present in his life since his childhood.

As his awareness of who his unfakeable, authentic being was increased, so did his love for his wife, and his desire to lead with authenticity. By complementing his consultation with my relationship breakthrough coaching sessions, both he and his wife learnt to be authentically present with each other. I helped them work through their relationship crisis and they learnt new ways of being, communicating, and transforming together. With time, the soulful relationship that was there when they got married, was now even more robust.

James became more energetic, focused and productive in the boardroom, and as he said in our last session, "Tony, I am delighted with what's happening in the bedroom too – thank you."

Just like James, for your love to be healthy, you need to be open to deconstructing your mind's hidden motives and meet your honest, trustworthy and loveable unfakeable being. Demonstrating adaptability, fragility, and vulnerability is what can help you create the kind of unconditional love that you know you deserve and want. The games that are played by the many warrior tough love personas day in and day out, are there to aid you in mastering the art of loving prudently.

Personally, the times I've felt the most intimate and the most loved by the people who I dated, were when we allowed each other's fragile, judgmental, and vulnerable personas express themselves authentically.

You are born to long for unconditional love. Yet, your warrior tough love persona makes you afraid of being judged, rejected, and unloved for who your unfakeable authentic individual indeed is. It is for this reason, that many of you put on the tough love mask to hide your flaws, fears, and insecurities from the people you desire to love and have in your life.

When you put yourself out there exactly as you are, many of you falsely think it leads to being rejected, and ultimately being hurt. That's the illusion your false persona wants you to believe in, and going through this persona integrating process you are learning throughout this book, you come to realize it is not others that are stopping love from finding its way to you. It is your expectation of others living outside of their authentic values, and inside of yours, that becomes the impenetrable shield that stops love reaching you. Travelling globally to consult individuals and businesses I get to meet a lot of people who have accomplished a lot in their careers and are now wanting to find love. Most of them had this impenetrable shield that stopped love from reaching them.

Equally, I observe how the loss of engagement, productivity, and profits in companies where I am asked to develop the companies' leaders and train their teams; is often the result of a lack of authenticity and the same disempowering and controlling behaviours you've been reading about.

That's why it is wise for you to know, that you must hone and own your tough love persona. It will free you from the need to protect yourself from the pain that comes from being rejected, judged, or unloved and it will make you face the truth and the love present in your unfakeable individual and in everyone you meet-authentically.

Love Yourself, as Everyone Else is Taken

To be loved for who you are, you must own all that you are. Otherwise, you start to second-guess what the other person likes or hates about you and you about them. This second-guessing and the non-accepting duality behaviour is just another dimension of your fierce, tough love persona that prevents you from attracting the prudential love you are seeking. When you don't love yourself, you build a shaky foundation based on what you think the other person is and wants, and you are both left questioning how to differentiate between the 'person' and the 'representative'.

One of the best things that happen as you start disarming the protective mechanisms of your tough love persona is that you become incredibly confident about telling people exactly who you are right away. If for instance, your goal is to be loved unconditionally, it's only logical to be your unfakeable self the minute you meet someone. While for some people confidence, truthfulness, and honesty may be the qualities they want from their partners, if the person you are trying to build a relationship with disowns these qualities in themselves, they will perceive you as arrogant, cocky, and off-putting and will kill any chance you may have with them.

This may be exactly your goal, to keep going on until you meet people who will love you for who you are, without the need to change something about you. So, your unfakeable being is the perfect screening tool your fierce warrior tough love persona can use to help you attract the unfakeable partner or friends you want in your life. Let the five-principles and everything you are learning transform the many fears, judgments, and illusions so that you can go on living life freely on your terms. Use them daily to love the unlovable in you and others while speaking and acting with integrity.

As the shield of your fierce warrior tough love persona's weakens, your guards go down, you start to build trust, you open up, and you truly let someone in. If you allow The Unfakeable Code® principles will guide you daily for you to create the intimacy, the fire, the desire, the trust, and the nurturing required to truly honour who your authentic, unfakeable being truly is and you will be loved for all that you are.

It is by being your true authentic self, the unfakeable you, that you create a solid foundation that is based on truth, trust and transformation of your masked personas into a genuine evolving individual. I recognize that for some of you, it can be hard to put yourself out there and test all you've been learning. The fear of rejection, abandonment, and being controlled may lead you to put on this fierce love warrior and start to fight the battle that your unfakeable persona already knows you have lost. You will find that continuing to play the game of your transient persona's, is the surest way to waste your most precious asset, your time. You'll remain emotionally unavailable, by portraying the energy that stops you from finding the unconditional love you crave.

It's only when you stop playing the games of your tough love persona and let your authentic, unfakeable being lead the way, that you will feel fulfilled, and you will find yourself in a nurturing, loving, and trustworthy relationship.

Many of you waste a lot of time with people in your life who don't love you as you are and expect you to change. The question you may want to answer right now is why? Why are you wasting time with the facades people show you that further strengthen the fierce, tough love warrior persona? What are you benefiting from in spending time to handle these relationships that can drain the life out of you?

When you find yourself in this kind of situation, here is something to remember:

Your greatest fear and your greatest desire are the same: to be seen, loved, and accepted for all that you are and are not. It's your perceived fears that prevent you from showing your true self. If you succumb to the fear, it will ensure that you'll never be seen or loved for who you are.

Surrendering to fear creates huge tensions, separations, and blockages in the energy of the heart, and your love becomes very conditional, transactional, and controlling in nature. You attract the wrong relationships, or you simply avoid being authentic because of the fear you have of being hurt, abandoned, and controlled.

Lack of love in your life can genuinely damage your general wellbeing. Without your self-love, you will not be able to unleash the power of your authentic being. You won't listen to your heart knowing, and you end up disconnected from the infinite wisdom that love is.

A talk I delivered to a group of executives called: **"How to Be Unfakeably Authentic and Get What You Want"** starts with Oscar Wild's famous quote. "Be yourself; everyone else is already taken." A simple yet powerful metaphor for the important role our authentic, and unfakeable self plays in leading, managing, and transforming the relationships we have with other people. You must learn to lead, live and love life authentically and not according to the judgments, opinions and expectations of others, but from the instructions coming from the king reining in your heart's kingdom – your soul.

When the voice of our unfakeable being is weak, your relationship will be in trouble, whether it is with your intimate partner, or with people you socialise with, work with or manage. Why? – because your masked deceptive personas make you believe that emotional intelligence is only about you being number one, and not giving a toss about other people.

Being unfakeable is the catalyst others who feel down can use to raise their emotional intelligence and take control of their own choices and perceptions in life. Both partners need an equal amount of emotional and spiritual knowledge to let this happen when the other partner is feeling down.

At some stage in your life, you'll reach a point where what's most important to you becomes true to your unfakeable individual. In doing so, you let your love be what unmasks all of the masked personas. You know this to be accurate, as it is what made you invest your money and time in reading this book because you put a value on your personal growth, on taking back control of the reins of your life to live authentically and freely on your terms.

I trust, that, at some point on our journey together you realized that your unfakeable individual could not be controlled by the temporary delight about some possession, work promotion, or the perfect house you have. None of those assets pays any attention to your secret longing for validation that your life has been worthwhile, that is has a meaning; but, it is driven by the power bestowed to you by your creator and your soul that loves the wholeness of you.

Think twice before you invest time in any kind of relationship that is based on need; for, with time, the other person will fade away, and if you're not careful, the void left behind will make you keep attracting the same type of relationships over and over again.

For your future self to thank you for the kind of personal, professional, business, spiritual, social, mental, emotional and financial relationship breakthroughs you want, make sure that the relationship you build in the moment are heart, trust, and values-based. Let your genuine unfakeable individual be the essential pivotal point – the crux – that determines whether the relationship you want to invest in will survive, die or flourish into becoming true love. Just like a lotus flower does when after years it emerges from the dirt it was planted in and rises and reaches the surface of the pond, and then blossoms beautifully.

Disarming your fierce warrior tough love persona is what you should be genuinely yearning for when you are dating and assessing potential partners or evaluating an existing relationship. If you're in a relationship and your partner is equally supportive and likes to challenge you – even if they don't actively encourage it – you'll probably remain with them. Why?

Because it is at the border of support and challenge that your unfakeable love will grow the most.

If your partner is not providing you with this support and challenge dynamic, many of you in this kind of relationships will get bored and move on. If you stay, at some point in your relationship, you begin to resent them. If you feel they blatantly hinder or stop your personal growth, you'll most likely seek to escape and create the freedom that your unfakeable evolving individual loves.

Many often seek others to help them grow, but very few of them do the work required to embrace the duality of each other's nature fully. This is why doing work where you feel challenged or supported is fulfilling. Or, for many of you who have children, you know how important it is in your children's upbringing to have a balance between supporting and challenging them. It is in maintaining this healthy dynamic that your unconditional love for them guides them to be all they are meant to become.

The only other thing that can validate you more than your tough love persona can is your unfakeable unconditional love – who loves who you are in your essence! If you have a partner who equally challenges and supports you, loves what you do and what you don't do, then you'll have an extraordinary love for one another – what most people know as true love.

Having this full love for one another will help you to win every battle that life has thrown at you both. It's in unleashing this power of your unfakeable self that your true love for one another can blossom. This kind of love for one another can quickly disarm your fierce warrior tough love persona.

Free your unfakeable love. Let love be the military commander that helps you to win every battle in life. It is with love leading the way that you can succeed in unimaginable ways.

The following exercise is designed to help you know more about your fierce love warrior, your tough-love persona role in your life; to assist you in identifying what causes the separation from your unfakeable self, and what the rejections you may be experiencing in your personal and intimate relationship say about you.

Answer the questions in as much detail as you can, for they'll help you on your journey to building a co-loving, trustworthy, and long-lasting relationship that you want to be in. Do the exercise as often as you need to help you to overcome what is stopping you from a loving partner coming along or being present in your life; to find clarity about whether you want to keep dating or stay in your existing relationship and keep learning more about each other. You also need to decide together whether it is worthwhile to continue to invest time in being with each other.

Above all, remember, the people who you work with, meet daily, have a relationship with, or are dating are merely there to help you to get to a place within yourself where you can identify, understand, and own not only your disowned parts of yourself but also remain non-judgmental for others to do the same.

- Choose in what kind of relationship you want to create a breakthrough, business, professional, social, family, personal or intimate.
- In as much detail as you can write down on a piece of paper, or in a word document what your description of love is and what it means to love and be loved by you and others?
- List your greatest fears about love, then for each concern, identify the content in your mind, and list as many unseen benefits you are getting from each of the perceived fears.
- What thoughts come to you by realizing that your partner doesn't 'complete' you?
- Do you find yourself needing to bargain or battle for power?
- What prevents you from being your true unfakeable self in a relationship, at work, or socially?
- What annoys you the most about the person you are with, the people you manage, are managed by or socialise with?
- Are you fascinated by the person you are dating, or do you put them in the pit? If so, write down the reasons why.
- Do you focus on deepening the connection with a partner through companionship and commitment to each other and developing a life together, or do you live fearing it will never happen?
- What outcomes would you create if you were open to share and connect to your innermost authentic self?
- Is being physically, mentally, emotionally and spiritually intimate vital to you? If so, what questions can you ask your partner that will help you to create the deeper connection that you are seeking?
- How important is feeling safe and secure with the person you are with to you?
- Will this person you are with, help you to grow and realize your dreams, hinder them – or both?

Now, the next step is to objectively look at what you have written and uncover the truths in which you feel alone, experiencing disconnection, and feel that you have to put on the tough love persona's mask. Is it on all levels, or is it specific? Use the list below to identify in which level you feel this way:

- Physically – are you satisfied with the frequency of physical giving and receiving, of love-making, and of being touched?
- Emotionally – are you emotionally honest and vulnerable with each other? How easily do you expand to the emotional aspects of love, intimacy, and the sharing of experiences?
- Mentally – do you communicate easily with one another or do you find it hard to share your true self? Do you anticipate each other's needs?
- Spiritually – do you have similar beliefs and attitudes to intangible things, such as personal growth?
- Financially – Do you feel that you are the breadwinner or are you equally contributing towards building financial security together?
- Relationship – Do both of you have a great relationship with yours and each other's authentic, unfakeable self?
- Love – Do both of you have similar knowledge of what real Love is? Do you practice support and challenge in equal measures when it comes to acknowledging each other's hierarchy of values?
- Business/Career – Are you loving what you do and even if you are not, do you allow yourself to support one another, and encourage people to love what they do? Are you adaptable to changing the career you may be in or investing in transforming the company you may be running?

Take your time to complete the exercise and to reflect on the answers you have just written before you move on to the final chapter. Make a list of all the things you might want to change, and make sure that next to each item you write its associated drawbacks and benefits.

Finally, create a robust love action plan your unfakeable individual can use in consciously creating the relationships you want to invest in and brag about to the world.

Let Your Authenticity Shape Your Destiny

"It is not in the stars to hold our destiny, but in ourselves." – William Shakespeare.

As a child, I grew up in a multicultural and multi-religious society where the majority of people believe that their destiny is predetermined by God. Often during my primary school days, I would question the adults who would tell me that my or their fate was determined by God. Why do they think it is so? What evidence do they have, and what would change in their lives if this weren't true?

The default answer I would repeatedly get is not to question God's words, which made me even more curious to ask them more questions. I would go on and ask them if what they are saying is true. Why did God give us the ability to think for ourselves, to make choices, and to learn? To again, be silenced by saying I'll be punished if I continue to question God's will.

This desire to question everything is what led me to this moment of writing this chapter for you, to inspire your unfakeable being by using all you've been learning to create your inspired destiny consciously.

The truth is, something or someone is going to shape your destiny one way or another. It may as well be you. Just like the above quote by Shakespeare, I believe, to a certain extent, that we have control over our destiny.

For many of you, the words 'destiny' and 'fate' may mean similar things. Still, for someone like me, who throughout life, kept questioning the unquestionable in the pursuit to find answers to life's greatest mysteries, they are distinctively quite different. Fate is what puts opportunities in front of us, but our destiny is ultimately determined by our brain. Our beliefs and ultimately, our hierarchy of values is what helps us make the choices and the decisions to create and shape our destiny.

For instance, if you go on holiday and you meet the perfect business partner, that was fate. But what you do about it what can shape your destiny. I am sure many of you would have experienced luck putting an opportunity in front of you, but you didn't seize it, and it passed you by. You may say to yourself that was destiny. Or perhaps some of you may have captured it and created a favourable outcome, and that new outcome was your destiny.

You exist as much in an abstract world as you do in a real, actual physical world. It is this symbolic world that makes us so different from other animals and what makes us develop ideas, beliefs, values, and philosophies. It is why we build countries and empires, and it is also why we express our creativity in different forms, some through business, leadership, entrepreneurial skills and others through music, art, and dance. The duality of our nature is the cause of much evil in the world, but it is also what motivates us to fight against it, produce meaning, and create an inspired destiny.

Discovering your unfakeability is an immortality project, so is the unfolding of your destiny through conscious and unconscious choice; that gives us a sense of meaning and purpose. It's most often a long-term effort to produce an inspired destiny that offers us lasting value, whether that be in the form of wealth, children, a book or a business that stands the test of time.

If you hold onto the idea of transient persona's self-importance objective, you'll end up pursuing immortality projects for shallow reasons that have to do more with a developed ego than the value your heart and your soul want to bring into this world.

By committing yourself not to an image of the transient personas you may have about yourself but to something transcendent beyond that, you get inspired to create a destiny shaped to be the divinity of your unfakeable being.

Rather than striving for fame, fortune, and a heroic identity, you are inspired to get there in service of something bigger, something more divine than you are as an individual. To some of you, this inspiration would be in the name of your loved ones, a parent who passed away, a cause you believe in, God, science or progress. For others, it would be out of the sheer joy, love, and reverence for a universal creative force.

I've seen how in the pursuit of a specific destiny that some of you fall into the trap of believing that you are more critical than your reality and the universe deems you to be. If you've invested a lot in your education, self-improvement, empowering and growing every crucial area of life, you'll be able to craft an authentic destiny shaped by your everyday actions, choices, and decisions in life.

Don't forget, many of you have different limitations on what you can and cannot undertake as a destiny project. Ensure that you shape it by means of what is important to you. You all have something that you value and would love to commit to creating, over a sustained period.

The realization of your destiny, whatever that may mean to you is deeply dependent by your values, beliefs, and what data is present in your psyche. Whether or not you realize it, it is continually shaped by the thoughts you produce, the language you use, and the consistent actions you take. Your authentic destiny is shaped by every choice and decision you make, and by what values you hold dear to your heart. It is those three things that also determine how you commit your money, time, energy and most importantly, who you become.

For many people, the destiny they create may be an amalgamation of the influences found in their surroundings. Still, for visionaries, who I am grateful to coach – their inspired destiny is born from going through a constant cycle of build and destroy. Like myself, many of these leaders and visionaries I work with are okay with acknowledging their lack of self-importance. Instead, they use the five principles to clarify their values, their vision and their commit to doing the work required to create an immortal legacy and destiny.

A lesson I learnt from creating different projects to support the vision to teach the principles and the methods that took me over thirty years to develop for the benefit of inspiring the lives of one billion people with people who are self-deceptive persona is the following:

To create a colossal destiny and realize your divinity's calling in life, make sure that you build authentic relationships based on integrity and invest money and time in projects that go beyond mere identity games and personal legacies. In creating an inspiring destiny project with people who are driven by the divine or the transcendent in them ensures that the meaning your vision carries is what propels everyone through life without getting detached from it.

I believe that it is our choices, decisions, and our hierarchy of values and actions, in response to what fate offers us, that matters and can help you consciously to create your desired destiny. Your destiny is not something you can sit by and let happen to you. It means taking action on the opportunities presented to you whereby you create, shape and evolve your destiny.

Remember, the only authentic individual you are destined to become is the one you decide and choose to be. You are here in this physical world to express your divinity, to learn lessons, to make hard decisions and to keep taking consistent actions that help you grow as humankind. Your destiny is therefore not something you can sit by and let happen to you. It is created by deliberate actions in alignment with being faithful to one's authentic self.

Remaining authentic in all that you do shapes your reality, your experiences in life, and ultimately; the freedom you create is the best way to determine the destiny that leaves an immortal legacy.

"If you do not change direction, you may end up where you are heading." – Buddha.

I was very fortunate to have a strict and soulful mother who made it easy for me to be authentic. Each time my frailties would bring me down, she would remind me of all the 'good stuff' I was bringing to the world. On so many occasions, when the tough would get going, she would remind me how my never-ending quest for answers would one day make me a great author, a destiny I have now created.

What I learnt while going through every hardship is that once you find inner peace, your heart and your soul will whisper to you your ever-evolving destiny. It is as you reach the intersection of what you are uniquely good at and what you love doing that the sky becomes the limit.

We are coming at the end of our journey together. Use the five-principles to evolve your authentic individual continually. In doing so, you can become better parents, teachers, scientists, business owners, and changemakers who get ahead in business and leadership.

Every exercise, each principle, and every choice and decision you make as a result of the upgrade in thinking you just received can help you authentically create an inspiring destiny, no matter what that may mean for you. If you want to get unstuck, ahead as a leader and as a lover, you want a calling for what you're doing, and you want to be authentically unfakeable.

THANK YOU for coming on this journey with me, now permit yourself to be the authentic you, the unfakeable you who is a masterful, free, powerful and worthy. Remember, it is in your moments of inspiration that your destiny is shaped.

Tony Jeton Selimi

P.S. You are born with the ability to do both evil and good; what you choose when war rages inside or outside of you is what defines the kind of unfakeable individual you become.

Who Can Benefit from Using The Unfakeable Code®?

Anyone can benefit from this stress-reducing, conflict resolving, leadership activating, life fulfilling and heart-opening behavioural change principles (BCP®) and code and use it as the most crucial life-changing tool. It is ideal for:

- CEO's, leaders, politicians, business owners, entrepreneurs, start-up owners.
- HR, communication, sales, marketing, and customer relations departments.
- Scientists, psychologists, psychiatrists, social workers, doctors, nurses, the NHS, and other health and wellbeing professionals and institutions.
- Life, business, leadership, executive and corporate coaches, financial specialists, mentors, healers, complementary therapist, personal trainers, consultants, and even international United Nations delegates and peace ambassadors.
- Parents, professors, teachers, children and students, educational institutions, prison workers.
- Film producers, directors, actors, musicians and artists.
- Anyone curious to learn more about living and loving authentically.
- Anyone seeking to emerge as an authentic individual and confident leader in their field.
- Anyone wanting to know how authentic living is the sincerest form of self-love that can help you leave an immortal legacy.

What next?

Instead of wearing masks, feeling stuck, powerless and out of control, and being disengaged and unproductive, you can choose to continue to evolve yourself into the unfakeable leader, teacher and the authentic individual you were born to be. It's now up to you to use all you've learned to be the creator, shaper, and master of your inspired destiny.

I'm overwhelmed with gratitude for developing this simple, yet valid five-step code born out of a culmination of more than forty years of research and studies in numerous disciplines including mathematics, engineering, technology, biology, physics, philosophy, theology, metaphysics, and psychology.

The Unfakeable Code® is a new and robust methodology for business, personal or professional transformation. It assists in upgrading your psychology and harmonising your body-mind-heart intelligence so that it can deal with any form of anxiety, conflict, and stress. It helps you see the hidden order that exists in all that life represents and diffuses judgments with objectivity so that you can develop more grateful states of love and vitality. It enables you to create inside-out authentic transformations that you as an individual, partner, parent, business owner, and leader are seeking.

After reading this book, you might feel inspired to keep in touch and to learn more about how my custom-created training and consulting using The Unfakeable Code® five-mind upgrading principles can turn your leaders into authentic, energised, and trustworthy individuals that Gen Z and future generations want to follow. Or you might perhaps invest in a business breakthrough immersion day that identifies and helps you to strategize how you can use authenticity as a powerful tool to grow your business and renew teams' performance, productivity, and sense of purpose.

Training your employees to be unfakeably authentic and instil empowering behaviours can get rid of the root cause of employee disengagement, organisation-wide distrust, burnout, and stress. Promoting authenticity increases your sales. It can help your sales team close faster on essential deals, or improve your HR team to put in place specific processes that will make it easier to attract and hire inspired employees that transform your organisational culture.

The five authenticity building and the ten behaviour changing principles can also be used to transform an underperforming, ageing healthcare system, tackle management, doctors and nurses' issues including internal conflicts, burnout, stress; as well as improve overall hospital staff's mental health. How about using the ten behavioural change principles to turn ageing educational structures to fit for purpose twenty-second century learning experiences?

Each principle can assist you to go deeper within your consciousness so that you can learn how to balance skewed perceptions using objectivity, intelligently use emotions, take back control and maximize your prime asset, 'you'. You now have a code and behaviour changing tool to help you best navigate uncertainty and to turn you into an authentic leader, lover, and changemaker who challenges the status quo.

It would be my honour to know you as you have taken the time to remember me. I love being of service to you, your family, business, institution, and country as I love contributing towards the evolution of human consciousness. Virtually or tete-a-tete, I love consulting clients like you from all over the globe, facilitating the realisation and the accomplishment of your business, personal and professional goals; provided you are ready to invest your energy, money and time in realising your highest vision.

Booking a breakthrough consultation can help you identify what you can do to jailbreak out of the prison of your mind, take back control of the direction your life is going in, and integrate your transient personas into an authentic, free and thriving individual; which will lead to increased confidence, more prosperous personal and interpersonal relationships, and an increase in your worth, influence and wealth.

It gives me tremendous joy to focus all of your mental faculties so that you can become an outstanding leader, entrepreneur, corporation, father, mother, son, expert and an individual who makes a visible impact. Each consultation, talk, and training can give you the clarity you need to turn a specific challenge into a steppingstone, and to harness your abilities to create and utilise your unfakeable creative force for the good of all.

Clarifying what you are inspired by establishes a healthy foundation for the growth you seek, and the purpose that nurtures your creative genius. Enjoy life's journey, not just the destination, welcome equally triumphs that inspire you and mistakes that depress you. Embodying this awareness is a significant part of your growth, of reaching a place of appreciation, gratitude, and sincere empathy. As you do this, inspiration will come to you when you least expect it. Any expression of your being that goes out to others can only touch their hearts when it comes from your unfakeable inner truth.

To take this work to the next level, you can download resources, take the unfakeability test, download my app, attend any of my events, seminars, talks, workshops, discussions, networking, retreats, or choose to accelerate your achievements by working with me privately.

To see what's coming up, connect with me on all social media channels, or to learn more on what my integrated work can do for you, please visit https://tonyselimi.com Remember to sign up to my inspirational newsletter so that you can receive information that inspires you to live a meaningful life, free resources, and year-round special offers.

Finally, to help others merge their transient personas into their unfakeable, authentic individuality, please review this book, so that together, we can evolve, grow and in turn transform the lives of One Billion people, so that they too can unleash the power of appreciation, gratitude, and love. And the best news is, you will be rewarded for taking the time to do so.

Here's how:

1. Write a review of this book.
2. Post it on Amazon, iTunes, Bookstore's website, Readers Digest, write it on your website's blog, share it on your Facebook page, Instagram, LinkedIn, and other mediums to be invented. If you are a journalist, do get in touch so that I can share in more detail how together we can educate and inspire your TV/Radio/Podcast audience, or interview me for a newspaper you may be writing for.
3. Share your review on Instagram and Twitter tagging @TonyJSelimi @TheUnfakeableCode, and send a screenshot of 'Verified Purchase' together with your review to info@tonyselimi.com.
4. As a thank you, you'll receive a free mp3 meditation you can use daily to energise your body-mind and automatically be entered into a regular monthly prize draw for the chance to win a one-hour breakthrough consultation worth £££.
5. If you have a favourite idea, sentence or principle, use it as a Tony J. Selimi quote in the book you may be writing, a talk you may be giving, and to ignite a desire in your heart,

inspire your loved ones, your social media fans and followers, your audience, and your colleagues and leaders!

Magic happens when objectivity becomes the default lens through which you observe reality. When you daily integrate traits of your transient personas and archetypes into your authentic individual, you become more authentic, focused, and unstoppable.

Make sure you use the principles as a way to unleash productivity, power and purpose in the domain of leadership, business, teamwork, and to pursue your personal, relationship, social and spiritual callings in life selflessly.

You will never be at peace with others if you are at war with yourself. Those who can see life with objectivity get to influence life.

Good luck!

Acknowledgements

A book is always a result of what is happening in our inner and outer reality. It would have been impossible to write this book without the love, support, and lifelong contribution by the thousands of people who have been part of my life since the day I was born. It has been assembled from years of learning and unlearning, overcoming one challenge after the other, and finding my calling, place, and role in the world.

The book embodies the years of study, research into different life disciplines and philosophies, and the knowledge acquired through consulting thousands of business owners and people from all professional backgrounds to help them break through addictions, fears, phobias, health problems, relationship problems, mental health crises and identity and leadership challenges; the books of thousands of authors I've studied, the writers of many of the blogs that I have read, the talks, workshops, and retreats I have held and the teachers' seminars I've attended.

Once in a while, a unique soul and a guardian angel comes into your life. For me, Dr. Sc. Todorche Stamenov is this kindred spirit; my soulmate who touched my heart, challenged me to my core and turned my world upside down. You are the wind beneath my wings that helps me fly to higher grounds so that I can fulfil my ever-evolving mission in life.

With your kindness, singing, childlike attitude and unconditional love, you healed my wounds you ensure and forever entertain my adventurous, freedom, and growth-seeking soul. Most of all, it is through your courage to go to work during the COVID-19 global pandemic to save many lives, that you also helped me focus so I could complete writing this book. In seeing how selflessly you give your all to help others live, you've taught me, our families, friends, and the nation the meaning of unconditional love. Thank you for all you do for others and for us. I love you for every moment we have shared, the good and the bad, every dance, smile, dining, cooking, exercising and travel experience we've ever had, for being a source of constructive criticism, immense inspiration, love and wisdom.

To my late parents Shaqir and Ljutvije Selimi and most avid supporters, thank you is not enough to describe the caring, devotion, strength, patience, and unconditional love you've shown me throughout our lives. Without all of the support and challenges you gave me, I would not be who I am today. Mum, you taught many life skills and the importance of speaking my truth. You created a healthy foundation in me of what love is, and is not, and you embedded the values that, to date, I embrace. Your life has been an inspiration not just to me, but to everyone who knew you. Dad, you ensured that I spoke a few languages, had the best education one could wish for, and taught me treasured business and entrepreneurial skills that prepared me for every storm life throws at me. You both dedicated your life's work for my siblings and me to have an education and a better chance for a healthy, meaningful, and fulfilling life.

Although the civil war separated us physically for almost ten years, I am blessed to have always had a spiritual and heart connection with you both that transcends time and space. I trust that my love, appreciation and gratitude to you both for all the love you have given me, is captured in this book, written with a heart calling to assist humankind in transcending to higher levels of consciousness.

This book is my way of honouring and appreciating you both, as well as our families, friends, clients, teachers, colleagues, journalists, event organisers, and you, the reader. It is a path that led me to create unimaginable breakthroughs that put me on the mission I am now on, which is, to travel globally and teach others what I have learnt so that more people can epitomise high human potential.

This is my gift to every human being who has ever felt the need to put on a mask to cover their unfakeable true self from the fear of being abandoned, rejected, and unloved at home, at work, or socially. To the many thousands of people who have been part of my journey, especially to my clients Tammy De Mirza, Mike Cicali, Chimene Van Gundy, Dr. Pietro Emanuele Garbelli, Paul McMonagle, Naip and Lumnije Morina, and Seli Canaj. To Joel, Timea, Sofie and Rodney Van der Molen for co-creating 'Living My Illusion – The Truth Hurts' multi-award winning documentary to share their coaching journey story so that others can benefit from the transformational teachings that took me over thirty years to develop, master, and now teach. Thank you to AnnaLynne McCord, Hollywood Actress and the Founder of TheLoveStorm, Yola Nash, Tuna Sejdi, Albanian singer and songwriter and all of my fans, readers, celebrity clients, family and friends.

I have been blessed to love and equally be challenged by extraordinary people, especially a big thank you to Joe Dispenza, Tony Robbins, Oprah, Nick Nanton, Steve Harrison, Barack and Michelle Obama, and Dr. John Demartini for inspiring me to expand my vision. Your teachings and methods have been a paramount factor for me to continue my quest for discovering life's truth and keep teaching what I learn to help others. Your lessons have given me a great confirmation that I am on the right track perusing and teaching others how by being authentically unfakeable, they too can expand their human and business potential. I thank you and love you.

Thank you to all the hundreds of people who have interviewed me on their TV, Radio and Podcast shows, as well as written about me in their magazines and newspapers. Especially my thanks go to Brian Tracy, Jack Canfield, Royal Correspondent Ian Pelham-Turner, Tyler Wagner, Ronnie Jacobs, Dr. Marina Nani, Sabrina Belsami, Frances Richards, Sara Troy, Besim Dina, Rudina Magjistrati, Nazim Rashidi, Zejxhane Osmani, Dardan Hoti, Haki Kika, Bashkim Hoti, Bashkim Reci, Ana Rustemi, Behare Bajraktari, Zana Muhaxhiri Ramadani, Qerim and Hanife Kryeziu, Artur Bejzade, Glori Janaj, Eni Dare, Zerijeta Jajaga, Avni Qahili, Niman and Valbona Hoxha, Helidon Kastrati, Eraldo Xhelili, Daniel Nikolla, Sarah-Anne Lucas, and every journalist who has interviewed and written about me.

Thank you all for your time, for what you do, and for the unwavering support to help me keep my promise to educate, inspire and transform your audience's perceptions so they can function at their best. Every conversation and interview have ignited an idea in your viewers', listeners', and readers' heads. It has saved lives and given hope to billions of people from all walks of life to be all they can be.

My thanks go to the millions of readers of my multi-award-winning and multi-times best-selling books A Path to Wisdom and #Loneliness, who took the time to share with me their breakthroughs, heart-wrenching stories and wrote Amazon reviews to inspire others, including Jellmaz Dervishi, Dr. Prof. Sulejman Abazi, Mouna Salih, Stuart Hall, Anna Orchard, Carl Tooney, and many other special people from all over the world who have supported me in this journey to bring and to share the message of love, healing, truth, equality, and the unfakeable way of living and leading.

This book would not have been possible without my reviewers Marie Diamond, Patryk Wezowski, Marija and Georgi Milushev, Andrew Priestley, The Hon Richard J Evans, Michael André Ford, Dije Berdyna, Adrian Dalipi, Ib Nielsen, Anila Gremy Krushova, Dr. Elgerta Ismaili, David Clive Price, Daniel Nikolla, Prof. Dr. Fadil Çitaku, Lisa White, Reziana Saiti, Albana Osmani,

Sue Bannister, Shelley J. Whitehead, and Fella Cederbaum. Thank you for daring, caring and for sharing your testimonials to help others grow.

A big thank you goes to my publisher and the entire team of experts for their capability and support needed to transform my manuscript and turn it into a life, business and leadership must-have guide, distributed to millions of people worldwide.

Thank you to everyone who attended, helped, performed, and supported me at my fiftieth birthday celebration and the global Amazon Prime Launch of Living My Illusion, especially to Theda Lehman, Tally Koren, the Albanian UK Ambassador, Qirjako and his wife Anxhela Qirko, members of the UK Albanian community, Erion Osmanaj, Juliana Shalla, Deborah Dollapi, Marjus Shushari, Adelina Toplica Badivuku, Roy Allaway, Rahil Abas, Vivek Dahiya, Denise Prentice, Ray Davis, Rodrigo Rayón, Sara Plasencia, Petar Todorov, Steven Jones, Nick and Jo Frank, Mariana Faria, Bianca Vuleta, Mirela Van Ejindhoven, Andrew Green, Marcello Gregorovic, Seba Bunjaku, Arben Osmani, Yuri Sharov, and Dianna Boner. Your turnout supported me with celebrating my birthday, life's work and Living My Illusion launch in style. I am honoured by your love, trust and in awe of your support for my calling in life and the vision for a better world. Through your presence, I have learnt to become a better listener and leader, allowing me to yield the knowledge and the wisdom that I now share with you and the whole world.

Thanks, are also due to many of you who are offering your own stories, recollections, and providing expert commentary and insights. Most of the people mentioned throughout my book have wholeheartedly shared their personal stories and have given me their permission to use their names. There are a few celebrity clients whose names I have deliberately changed or whose identities have been withheld to safeguard their privacy. Please accept my gratitude, anonymously.

This book would not have been possible without the many long hours, commitment, consistency, sleepless nights, the sacrifices, and the discipline required for my mind, body, soul and heart to work in synchronicity so this book could come to fruition. Thank you, and I love you.

Finally, may the rippling effect of The Unfakeable Code® five life-transforming principles and ten behavioural change principles teachings be passed on from generation to generation — so as a species we can safeguard the sanctity of human life as we venture into space and make new waves.

About the Author

Born in 1969 in the town of Gostivar, Republic of Northern Macedonia, Tony J. Selimi moved to London in 1990 at the age of twenty to find a haven from the atrocities of the civil war in which he had to fight. Like a phoenix rising from the ashes, he went from living homeless and penniless to becoming an internationally recognised leader in personal development, a professional speaker, an award-winning author, and business coach, specialising in human behaviour, emotional intelligence and leadership performance.

For over fifteen years, he contributed to leading and managing multi-billion-pound technology programs in the private and public sectors. In 2009, after facing another life-transforming crisis, redundancy, he decided to start his own business and pursue his heart's calling; to travel the world and teach others how to find the answers and solutions to life's obstacles, cope better with their daily business, leadership and personal demands and pressures.

Tony specialises in assisting people in breaking through mental imprisonment, addictions, phobias and limiting beliefs to awaken their inner leader, maximise their human potential and accomplish higher levels of achievement. Like a transparent mirror, he is known for his ability to see through people's problems, behaviours, thought patterns, values and disempowering beliefs to help them rid themselves of lies that conceal their unfakeable, and authentic individual that is powerful, truthful, and worthy.

The experience of working in the corporate world, overcoming many personal and professional challenges, as well as coaching many people from all walks of life, gives him unique insight into the pressures, challenges, and magnitude of issues his clients, including Fortune 500 CEO's, Authors, Entrepreneurs, Managers, Consultants, Sales People, Scientists, Doctors, Royalty, Film and TV stars, and Politicians, to name a few.

Senior Executives of companies such as Microsoft, Apple, Facebook, SAP, Bank of America, Ignis Asset Management, Deutsche Bank, Ernst & Young, Santander, Vandercom and Mishcon de Reya across EMEA, Asia and USA seek his help to improve their business performance, grow their leaders, engage employees, and increase team performance, productivity and profitability. He creates custom-made training and consulting to help businesses mindfully implement change programs, mental health, diversity and inclusion, and wellbeing strategies.

It is through proven processes that Tony assists people in building the strong foundations and emotional resilience needed to create amazing and lasting spiritual and material transformations.

Tony is a University College London (UCL) graduate who studied many life disciplines and received several awards. He is a qualified coach recognised by several reputable institutions, including the International Coaching Federation (ICF), the Institution of Leadership and Management (ILM), the Demartini Institute, the Complementary Therapists Association, Martin Brofman's Foundation of Advanced Healers and he is a certified Reiki Master Teacher.

As the beloved author of A Path to Wisdom and #Loneliness, Fit for Purpose Leadership #3 and The Unfakeable Code®, he crafted the Behavioural Change Principles®, and the TJSeMethod: ALARM®, a one of a kind modernised formula for health, wealth and fulfilment, that has been hailed as the new self-improvement tool, now containing the most potent principles to maximising business, leadership, and personal potential known to humankind. His self-mastery values-based methods, principles and strategies create the life outcomes people intuitively know they deserve.

Globally, Tony travels to educate and inspire people with enlightening perspectives, humorous metaphors, and a heart-illuminating personal journey. He provides answers to questions and gives practical solutions to life's challenges in one to one consultations, talks, workshops, corporate training, mastermind groups, Vital Planning Advanced Learning retreats, inspirational articles for Newspapers and Magazines, as well as through regular contributions to diverse media outlets, high-profile blogs, TV programmes, podcasts, YouTube Videos, Books (print, digital, audio, video), The Unfakeability Index Test, apps, social media, Udemy courses and downloads of his TJS Evolutionary Meditation Solutions®.

He has spoken on grandiose stages such as the United Nations, Rotary International, the Cranfield School of Management, International Film Festivals, the London Business Show. His TEDx talk Technological Armageddon: A Wakeup Call watched by millions of people addresses the present and future challenges we will face as well as the opportunities we will create in the next ten to 100 years, with the rise of artificial intelligence.

His work also includes Films and Documentaries, such as the Multi-Award-Winning Living My Illusion on Amazon Prime, and has appeared on over 500 radio and TV stations across the world, including interviews by Royal Correspondent Ian Pelham-Turner, Besim Dina on Oxygen TV, Top Channel Albania, by Jack Canfield and Brian Tracy in America and on SKY, ABC, NBC, CBS and FOX, reaching over 100 million viewers, listeners and readers worldwide.

Tony founded TJS Cognition and is a founding partner of the multi-award-winning media company, Living My Illusion, with a heavenly vision to infiltrate his methods, principles and teaching in business, leadership, government, education and health care. In doing so, he aspires to inspire a decisive action in the lives of one billion people by 2030, and contribute towards the accomplishment of the UN's 17 Sustainable Development Goals and the evolution of human consciousness.

He promotes the importance that heart, values and service-driven leadership, entrepreneurship, personal self-mastery and spiritual development play in our wellbeing, the future of work, healthcare, education, and governance. Tony loves researching and teaching topics that bridge science, business, wealth building, psychology, energy healing, wellbeing, time, space, miracles and belief.

As a NOHE/UN World Ambassador of Children in Excellence, Equality, and Positive Role Model, he uses his hard-earned fame and influence to promote the importance coaching, mindfulness, and meditation on our personal and professional lives, in our communities, family, society, and universally.

No matter who you are or where you are from, this is your time to access your inner knowing, plan and transform your reality. Tony is known for assisting you to create transformational business, professional and personal breakthroughs; leaving you with a sense of inner peace and feeling elevated, inspired and priceless.

To connect, follow and obtain further information on what Tony can do for you, your family, your audience, business, country, leaders, teams and organisation, please visit https://tonyselimi.com.

Transformational Products

A Path to Wisdom

Distractions prevent you from listening to the inbuilt ALARM that your body uses to alert you when something is wrong. Ignoring the body's wisdom is the root cause of disease, faster ageing, fears, business and personal failures, as well as many psychological disorders. Life adversities have the power to bring you out of your natural state of healthy balance, and into creating lower mind animal behaviours that prevent you from realizing your highest expression of yourself.

Judgment of self and others is the biggest killer on the planet, but what if you could go from lower mind reactive thinking into a Divine being who is objective, proactive, and transcends human traits for a higher purpose that elevates your current awareness? What would be possible for you then?

This Amazon bestselling and multi-award-winning book is a timeless life manual that offers a road map that safely guides you through an inside-out reflective journey to find and address the root cause of your physical, mental, emotional, spiritual, financial, business, relationship and self-love, self-worthiness, and self-confidence issues, that keep you out of your healthy natural state of inner balance – empowering you to activate, advance and accelerate your human and business potential.

In a volume that won the Top Shelf Magazine Indie Book Award, the Book Excellence Award, the Finalist Award in the USA Book Contest, got over one hundred sterling Amazon reviews and was given readers favourite ten-star seal, you'll find hidden an ocean of wisdom waiting for you to discover it.

You will learn how to use TJSeMethod: ALARM® to help you acknowledge, listen, act and respond to your inner voice that is there to guide you to take back the reins of your life and to harness the healing power of unconditional Love. Doing all the exercises with a childlike curiosity assists you to use your innate intelligent built-in faculties to deepen your understanding of yourself, awaken you to your true calling, and honour your spirit, greatness and wisdom.

This proven method developed through thirty years of heartfelt research can assist you in establishing an easy path to healing and transforming every critical area of your life. Complete the exercises in the book and use the twenty-five conscious creating principles embedded in the method to learn how to:

- Acknowledge and own your power, be more assertive, influential, and in control of your choices and decisions.
- Love the duality of your nature, heal your body, mind and soul and listen to your body's wisdom.
- Achieve higher states of awareness, and intelligently use all of your faculties.
- Create results, live in harmony with your authentic values and your life's purpose.
- Attract abundance, opportunities and miracles into your life.

Learn, apply, and use the TJSeMethod: ALARM® twenty-five principles to empower, grow and transform all of the eight critical areas of your life: For more information, please visit https://www.amazon.co.uk/Tony-Jeton-Selimi/e/B00KXBZSX0

#Loneliness: The Virus of Modern Age

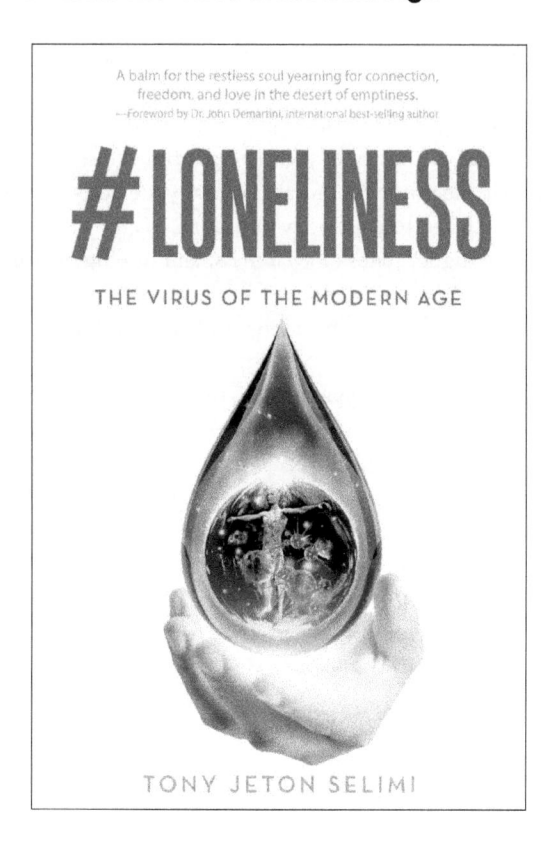

So connected, yet desperately we are alone, drowning in an ocean of infinite possibilities.

Meticulously researched and written, #Loneliness: The Virus of the Modern Age explores the fierce scientific, psychological and spiritual impact of loneliness – a problem that has become an ironic epidemic in a world that is more interconnected than ever before.

In a world where communication is instant, where billions of people can interact at just a moment's notice, it will come as a shock to many to learn that loneliness is an epidemic more rampant and destructive than at any point in history. Almost everyone faces adversity from the isolation that causes us some degree of depression, anxiety or diminished self-esteem.

We have become accustomed to a new way of being alone together in a technological cocoon, that covers up our real pain. Our true essence is hidden behind façades that we show to the world from the fear of being judged, criticized, and rejected. This is what brings us out of a natural state of healthy balance, is the root cause of disease, and what creates the segregation experienced worldwide.

#Loneliness is a global call for people to redefine themselves in the face of life's most significant challenges. Comforting, moving, and spiritually practical, this book is a guide to help you break through your apparent loneliness, and shift you toward crowd-nurtured world peace and the next stage in our evolution.

Loneliness not only disintegrates your mental and physical health, but it also infects your genome and leads to multiple changes while painting a dark and negative picture of the world around you. The most surprising thing to learn is that today's obsession with technology does nothing more than simply awaken the segregation, discord, and loneliness already inside us all, which further spirals our moods and our outlook.

Read this book to make you aware of that problem, create a road map that safely guides you out of your disempowered states, and empower yourself to redefine the meaning of your life, so that you can overcome adversity with ease and build the happiness and prosperity you so deeply crave.

Use it to reveal how inner discord creates your deceptive loneliness, which is spontaneously appearing around the world, in the form of war, racism, nationalism, xenophobia, homophobia, illness, high divorce rates, financial crises, and so much more. It is a life manual that shows you how to extract wisdom from every adversity, so that you can become a more balanced, mindful, and heart-centred individual, leader, parent, teacher, and human being.

If you let it, each page will guide you and encourage you to make the changes that your soul is craving. The principles and ideas shared will teach you how to listen to your heart in ways you didn't know were possible, amplify your awareness and ultimately break free of the cocoon that is stopping you from seeing and embracing the beauty of this world.

It goes beyond you as individuals; it will teach you how to unite and ignite humanity's collective voice so that we can progress to the next stage of our evolution. If this is you calling, then get this book from https://www.amazon.co.uk/Loneliness-Virus-Modern-Age/dp/1504343999

Fit for Purpose Leadership #3

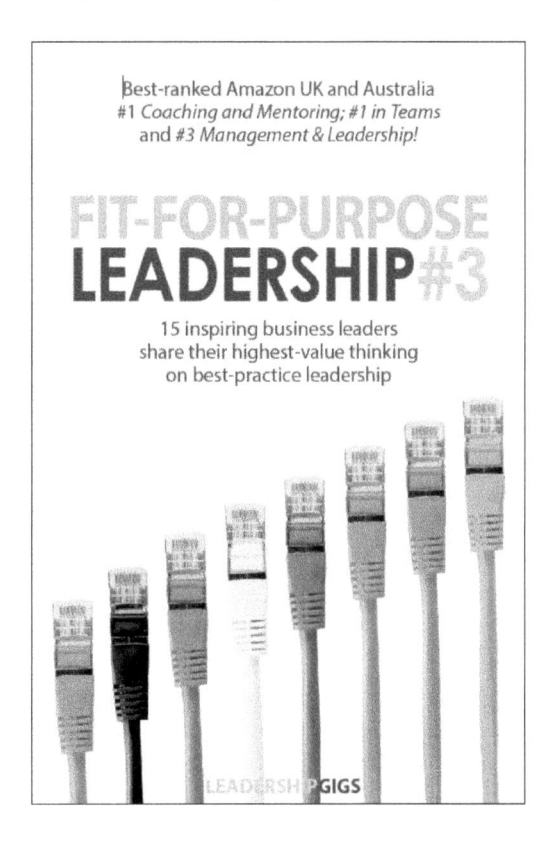

Burnout is a significant personal and public health problem. Burnout presents itself in many forms, but the most significant one is in the way of the overworked employee stretched thin by too many responsibilities, too little training, too few resources and too little time. In fact, according to some researchers, burnout has several faces.

In its third outing, in Fit For Purpose Leadership #3, together with fifteen high performing leaders from around the world, we share our highest-value thinking and advice on business leadership, with a focus on health, mindset, social and relationships, meaning and purpose, best practice and emerging trends.

I wrote a chapter on burnout, as globally, I consulted many business leaders who asked me to help them to cope better with this growing problem. In this chapter, you'll learn how to be aware of the triggers, varieties of exhaustion, and of how different symptoms require different solutions.

With a client example, you are taken on a journey on how you can counteract this kind of burnout through clarifying leaders' and organisation-wide values, aligning those values with a clear vision, and giving employees clear and realistic goals and advising what they need to meet those goals, and offer appreciation for a job well done.

In the chapter, I share how by tackling burnout successfully, you can also get rid of the problem of high absenteeism, low engagement, exhaustion, stress, and mental health issues that may otherwise arise.

If you want to create an environment that allows employees to thrive and flourish, will promote excellent mental health and build a healthy organisational culture, then everything the other leaders and I share in this leadership-focused book will help you to create a meaningful and rewarding workplace that guards you and your employees against burnout.

Grab your copy from https://www.amazon.co.uk/gp/product/B07BRXF5FZ

Living My Illusion – The Truth Hurts Multi-Award Coaching Documentary

In the Facebook/Instagram world everyone thinks that Joel has made it. But when he invites a famous life coach and Human Behaviour expert Tony J. Selimi into his world, a journey of self-discovery reveals the truth, leading to a decision that will change the course of his life. A morally provoking, contextually interesting, and life-transforming true story of how a successful entrepreneur, husband and father is willing to do what most people fear to do; but deep down, they wish they could do themselves.

Through shocking truth-telling interviews and private one-on-one coaching sessions, you can see Joel's 'in the moment' realisations during an original series of revealing questions by Tony, bringing him to question the realities of the life created by the masked personas he shows to the world.

Joel courageously shares deep and personal learnings, speaking honestly about resulting to IVF to conceive a child, sexual repression, and wondering if he ever loved his wife at all. He does this without fear of any backlash. Should he succumb to the expectations of his father, what his friends are doing to get back in line, or follow the feeling burning inside him, at the cost of hurting his loving wife?

This timely documentary about the toxic personal, family and business effects of midlife crisis and how Tony's Transformational Life Coaching and integrated approach can help people to be true to themselves, makes a case for breaking certain taboos and adds friction from a moral standpoint.

In each snapshot of the real coaching session, you'll see how Joel is trying to work out what the illusion of fame, fortune and freedom means to him, at the expense of his health, business and marriage. From the other aspect, you'll learn from Tony's unique guidance, teachings and wisdom, how you, as the viewer can become aware of the subject's resulting actions and the midlife crisis saga that no one can escape.

Living My Illusion-The Truth Hurts, co-created by Joel, Timea and Tony, pushes the boundaries of the documentary form, being a mirror to every person, inviting you to self-reflect on the lies you tell, the truths you conceal, and the fearful or courageous decisions you make. You'll realise how questioning every societal value you uphold can help you to live an authentic, inspired, and fulfilled life.

In Tony, Joel has found someone to give him the clarity he needs at a crucial point in his life, to help him find his unique voice and choose a path to living a purposeful life, thus giving to his wife and family the greatest gift he could ever give, to have Tony as their teacher to help them find their truth and ultimate freedom.

Since completion, Living My Illusion was declared: the New York City Independent Film Festival – Official Opening Night Film, a Platinum Winner of International Screen Awards and Cardiff International Film Festival. It was: a Winner of Huston International Film Festival Award, Impact DOCS Awards, Los Angeles Film Awards, Hollywood International Documentary Awards, Docs Without Borders, Barcelona International Film Festival, Amsterdam International Filmmaker Festival, Nice International Film Festival, Madrid International Film Festival, Milan International Filmmaker Festival, UK Monthly Film Festival, Oniros Film Awards Italy Finalist and Rome Independent Prism Awards – Official Selection.

Watch Living My Illusion on Amazon Prime Video http://bit.ly/LMIAmazon, do leave your review, and share it with someone you know who is going through a midlife crisis and is in need of clarity.

TJS Evolutionary Meditation Solutions®

There is growing scientific research on the effects of mindfulness and meditation practices. The results are coming in, and they are showing that they help you to sleep better, feel more energised, heal your body faster, make more rational decisions, and most importantly, they change the shape of your brain.

Imagine what you could achieve if, in your mind, you had access to a Star Trek Enterprise holodeck where you could play any possible simulation that instructs your subconscious mind to create a whole new reality for yourself.

This is what inspired Tony J. Selimi to create TJS Evolutionary Meditation Solutions®, a set of guided meditation exercises that help you to relax, heal, get creative, get energised, get innovative, and offer you a way to become alive, focused and beautiful inside-out.

Each meditation will take you on a more profound inner journey to unlock your true potential. Committing to doing at least one meditation daily, will help you open up multidimensional awareness, healing capacities, develop your intuition and experience an expanded version of you.

Use them together with A Path to Wisdom, #Loneliness, and The Unfakeable Code® books to accelerate your journey to be unfakeable with, and increase your awareness of your relationship with all that is. You can use them at home, at work, in the park, and when you travel, to unveil the true beauty that waits for you inside you.

Give yourself the gift you always wanted, the gift of stillness, self-love, and self-awareness of the Divinity of your infinity. Meditating before you go to work, when on your break, or before you go to bed will help you transmute any negative-energy into satin-white purity, and keep your energy and vibration levels high. As you feel your inside shifting, what you attract in your life will shift. This is a joyous co-created experience in which you'll have a lot of fun redesigning your reality.

Your mind wants you to feel good, deep down, you want to feel good about you, but your brain is busy, trying to make you feel good in other things. No more excuses, now you can use daily TJS Evolutionary Meditation Solutions® to help you heal your body-mind-heart, activate your inner doctor, relieve emotional and physical pain, create inner peace, energise your body, and so much more.

To download them on iTunes, use the following links:

http://bit.ly/MeditationToBeAMoneyMagnet;
http://bit.ly/MasterYourEmotions;
http://bit.ly/BlissfulMind;
http://bit.ly/AwakenYourInnerDoctor;
http://bit.ly/AwakenYourHeart;
http://bit.ly/TransformDailyNegativity

You can also download them as an album from Tony's website. To be kept informed when a new meditation is available, please sign up to receive his educational, inspirational, and promotional newsletter at https://tonyselimi.com

Vital Planning for Elevated Living

If you are ready to invest five-days in experiencing an ultimate personal and business growth adventure – then the Vital Planning for Elevated Living life-enhancing, mind calibrating and heart-opening symposium is a choice your future self will thank you for.

It is an exclusive opportunity to have Tony J. Selimi, one of the world's most respected teacher, leading elite life coach, and business mentor who specialises in human behaviour all to yourself to create the breakthroughs you desire, deep down. He will help you dissolve emotional charges, answer all your questions, and teach you how to use The Unfakeable Code®'s five mind upgrading codes, ten behavioural changing principles (BCP®) and the twenty-five mind conscious engineering principles of TJSeMethod: ALARM® to realise your human and spirit potential.

It is a fully customised and flexible learning experience held in beautiful locations around the world, so that you can focus on what is most important to you. You can use this time to build an inspiring vision, clarify your purpose in life, give birth to original work, start, grow and expand your business, become a confident leader, speaker, successful author, or create a step by step plan to empower all of the critical areas of your life.

This is your opportunity to transform any challenge you are currently facing by working it through with Tony. Previous clients have mentioned how quickly he got to the heart of the matter, helped them identify what was holding them back from being inspired and successful in life, and provided a resolution that turned their specific challenges into stepping-stones.

Whether you are facing financial, family, emotional, leadership, health or business challenges – he will give you personal and powerful insights that will transform undesirable situations into favourable outcomes.

It is an exceptional advanced learning experience designed for successful, committed and high aiming entrepreneurs, business owners, leaders, celebrities, influencers and other change-makers who are committed to living an authentic life and being of service to others at a level few have ever imagined.

For more information, client testimonials, please go to https://tonyselimi.com/vital-planning-retreat/

Notes

Rate this book on our website!

www.novum-publishing.co.uk

novum PUBLISHER FOR NEW AUTHORS

The publisher

He who stops getting better stops being good.

This is the motto of novum publishing, and our focus is on finding new manuscripts, publishing them and offering long-term support to the authors.
Our publishing house was founded in 1997, and since then it has become THE expert for new authors and has won numerous awards.

Our editorial team will peruse each manuscript within a few weeks free of charge and without obligation.

You will find more information about
novum publishing and our books on the internet:

w w w . n o v u m - p u b l i s h i n g . c o . u k